The secret of how to win
Freedom from clutter!

DON ASLETT

D0767508

First published in Great Britain
in 1985 by **Exley Publications Ltd,**
16 Chalk Hill, Watford,
Herts WD1 4BN, United Kingdom.
Reprinted May 1986
Reprinted January 1987
Reprinted March 1989
Reprinted August 1990

Copyright © Don Aslett, 1984

British Library Cataloguing in
Publication Data

Aslett, Don.
    The secret of how to win freedom from clutter.
    1. Conduct of life.
    I. Title.
    158'.1   BF637.C5

ISBN 1-85015-028-1 (h/b)
ISBN 1-85015-056-7 (p/b)

First published in the USA
by Writer's Digest Books.

Printed and bound in Great Britain by
Guernsey Press Co. Ltd., Guernsey, Channel Islands.

We (my favourite housekeeper and I) dedicate this book
to Gladys Allen, who ironed out the wrinkles and
removed the cobwebs from the script.
    We also give our sweeping thanks to John Preston
Creer who waxed the idea of the book, to Clark Carlile
who dusted away any doubts we could do it, to Ernie
Garrett and Anne Montague who mopped up the
English, to Mark Browning who polished the style, and
to artist David Lock who decorated the pages.

ILLUSTRATIONS BY DAVID LOCK

Contents

Preface: OK . . . I'll confess first		6
Introduction		9
1	Junkee ID test	11
2	The genealogy of junk	16
3	A hundred and one feeble excuses for hanging on to clutter	20
4	Junkosis	26
5	The economy of clutter	30
6	Home sweet home . . . full of junk!	37
7	Personal treasures	51
8	Taming the paper tiger	61
9	Dress less for success	74
10	Junk on wheels	81
11	Junk danger zones	86
12	You *can* take it with you — but don't	93
13	Hooked on excess luxuries	98
14	Destroying your body with junk	109
15	People can be junk?	118
16	How to leave it and love it (clutter)	127
17	Let's get started on your clutter	134

OK...
I'll confess first.

I grew up in a family that always believed in keeping all kinds of junk just in case it might come in useful for something.

Keeping stuff still seemed reasonable as I grew older. When my drawers, shelves and cupboards were filled, I followed other people's examples and got more drawers. I built more shelves — and raised my bed so there was more room under it for storage. Then I left home for college, and when junk pushed me out of my room, I finally began to see sense. My junk took up all my living space, and if I was going to do any living, I'd have to clear it out.

Clearing clutter and junk out of my life was so exhilarating, I began to clear up other people's clutter, dirt and junk. I organized my own cleaning company, and over the next eight years, built it into a national operation.

During this time, thousands of people brought their clutter and cleaning problems to me. In an attempt to offer a solution, I wrote a book entitled *Is There Life After Housework?* To my surprise, it soon became an international bestseller.

Because I had become aware that a good fifty per cent of housework was not just sweeping, dusting and polishing, but involved shunting clutter, litter and junk from place to place, I included a chapter called 'Out with Junk' in *Is There Life After Housework?* Its basic message was that getting rid of stuff you don't need is the easiest way to free yourself from household imprisonment.

The response to this chapter was overwhelming. In the more than 600 radio, television and newspaper interviews I did in the next two-and-a-half years, my readers' and listeners' most intense interest was in junk. Phone calls, letters and live audiences throughout the U.S. and England — even celebrities — willingly confessed their clutter and how

it had negatively influenced their lives.

Before long, whenever I went to do an interview or make an appearance I would end up expounding less on cleaning secrets and efficiency and more on the art of clearing out junk. Everyone wanted me to tell them how to spot, sort, get rid of and/or hide their junk. I discovered that people suffer acute guilt because of the useless belongings that clutter their lives. I found that everyone of us is a hoarder and that it's the single biggest reason for personal unhappiness.

My enthusiasm to produce a book became uncontrollable; I had collected so much information and so many impressive testimonials on de-junking and I *had* to write it.

I hope you'll find *Freedom from clutter* sheds some light on junk and its damaging effects. Some of the information and opinions might bite a little, but please don't be offended. My only intention is to help you improve the quality of your life.

Don G. Aslett

Introduction

Life *is* pretty good, isn't it? We might have a few stresses and strains, but on the whole we're safe and well fed and sheltered, surrounded with plenty, comfort, luxury, convenience and freedom. We can, one way or another, attain the pleasures, places and things we want — when and where we want them. Most of us do just that — attain, accumulate, collect — enough is never enough. The more we get the more we want.

The crunch comes when we realize that all that comfort, convenience and *stuff* costs. We have to pay for it, keep track of it, protect it, clean it, store it, insure it and worry about it. This takes energy and effort (in fact, a great part of our lives). Later we have to move it, hide it, apologize for it, argue over it.

It stifles us and robs us of freedom because so much of our time is needed to look after it. We have no time to have fun, to do the things we really want to do. Not only are our houses, drawers, cupboards and vehicles so crowded that we can't breathe, but our minds, emotions and relationships, too, become dull and stagnant. We're so surrounded with stuff, we don't even have time for the people who mean the most to us.

Finally — often too late — we realize that most of that which has surrounded us, choking out good living, squeezing the physical and emotional life out of us, is just junk — *clutter*.

Millions of us have reached this stage, with feelings and sensitivity gone. Our life not only seems to be but *is* swallowed up. We don't own ourselves any more; we feel smothered and depressed.

Getting the clutter out of our lives can and will rid us of more discouragement, tiredness and boredom than anything else we can do.

There really is a solution

In this book I will try to help you:
1. Learn to identify junk and clutter, since *you* are the one who ultimately has to do something about it.
2. Realize what clutter is doing to you personally.
3. Gain some practical instruction on de-junking.

Start now

I promise you no recipe, remedy, reorganization or rebuilding plan will renew you like the simple, easy, inexpensive process of de-junking. I hope you'll find this book the catalyst you need to get the job done.

Chapter 1

Junkee ID test

Circle the answers nearest to the truth and jot down your score.	More than I'll ever admit to	More than I'd like	Only a few things	None	Score
1. If my cupboards and drawers were searched right now, how much junk would be found?	1	2	3	5	
2. I own clothes and shoes that won't fit or are ugly or hopelessly out of style.	1	2	3	5	
3. I save old uniforms or maternity/ baby clothes I don't need any more.	1	2	3	5	
4. I hoard odd socks or tights with one laddered leg.	1	2	3	5	
5. I own costume jewellery and badges that I never wear (for good reason).	1	2	3	5	

	More than I'll ever admit to	More than I'd like	Only a few things	None	Score
6. I save colognes and after-shaves I can't stand the smell of, or make-up I tried and don't like.	1	2	3	5	
7. My medicine chest holds bottles of ancient vitamins and antique prescriptions.	1	2	3	5	
8. I have empty, non-returnable or other honestly useless bottles inhabiting my house.	1	2	3	5	
9. I keep plain old ordinary empty boxes.	1	2	3	5	
10. I have old wedding announcements, greeting and Christmas cards squirrelled away from acquaintances I scarcely recall.	1	2	3	5	
11. I save left over scraps of crumpled Christmas wrapping paper that I never use.	1	2	3	5	
12. I keep unread circulars and lapsed driver's licences, expired policies and passports.	1	2	3	5	
13. I cut out coupons and special offers for products that I never buy.	1	2	3	5	
14. I've kept books I couldn't force myself to finish and magazines that are more than a year old.	1	2	3	5	

	More than I'll ever admit to	More than I'd like	Only a few things	None	Score
15. How many unused recipe cards/cookery books/do-it-yourself manuals do I have?	1	2	3	5	
16. I store old paint (half tins or less), stiff brushes and matted rollers.	1	2	3	5	
17. I have old curtains or blinds stashed away that I've dragged around from past houses.	1	2	3	5	
18. I have machinery, gadgets and appliances that don't work or have parts missing.	1	2	3	5	
19. I have wristwatches or clocks that aren't working.	1	2	3	5	
20. I have furniture and other items I am going to mend, sell or strip some day.	1	2	3	5	
21. I keep old patterns and scraps of wool and material that will probably never be used.	1	2	3	5	
22. I have paraphernalia from hobbies, projects and classes I started and 'may some day take up again.'	1	2	3	5	
23. I save every drawing my children ever did, and all their school reports since the year dot.	1	2	3	5	

	More than I'll ever admit to	More than I'd like	Only a few things	None	Score
24. I have keepsakes but I can't remember what sake they were kept for.	1	2	3	5	
25. I have photos I seldom look at because they're stashed away and hard to find.	1	2	3	5	
26. I have souvenirs or knick-knacks that I dust, clean, store and abhor.	1	2	3	5	
27. I keep toys (adult or children's) that are broken, outgrown or not used.	1	2	3	5	
28. I have old games and puzzles with pieces missing.	1	2	3	5	
29. The boot, floor and glove compartment of my car are filled with old torn maps, inoperative torches and sweet papers.	1	2	3	5	
30. When someone visits my home, how many excuses does my junk seem to call for?	1	2	3	5	
31. If someone gave me £1 for every piece of junk I have, how much money would I get?	1	2	3	5	
				TOTAL	

Your Junkee test score

30-60	**96-130**
THE END IS NEAR. . . You're in trouble. Read *Freedom from clutter* three times, gird your loins and start de-junking ruthlessly. You might possibly survive your junk.	THERE IS HOPE. . . If you can clean up/come to terms with those few problem areas, clutter won't have a chance to spread.
60-95	**131-150**
YOU'RE ON THE BRINK. . . If you start to de-junk today, you can make it. Read *Freedom from clutter* and commit yourself to do it.	YOU ARE PURE. Read *Freedom from clutter* to perfect yourself and then pass it on to a junkee friend or relative.

Chapter 2

The genealogy of junk

Where did our clutter inclinations come from? Were they inherited, absorbed, evolved, hatched, home-grown? Perhaps all of these things or perhaps Adam, when commanded to multiply and replenish the earth, thought that possessions were included in the instructions.

For centuries people have hoarded, fought for, lied for, died for objects that mostly were or became worthless junk. Junk soon became more important to mankind than clean air, beautiful land, pure love and total freedom. You and I are the procreators of junk.

So clutter began with our uncontrollable desire to have more, better, bigger things — even if they aren't good for us, even if we really don't want them, need them or have a place for them. Enough is never enough!

Don't feel guilty — almost every single one of us, deep in our hearts, would like to be able to poke around a junkshop unidentified. We want more, no matter how much we have of our own; even if ours is a better quality than our neighbour's, we want theirs. The lust to have things is a drive almost equal to hunger and sex. *Coveting thy neighbour's clutter is the seed of all junk acquisition.*

Your junk drive is to blame

Notice how many jumble sales and car boot sales are going on (generations of junk are finally pushing people out of their houses). It isn't that they need the money — only fifty things are sold out of two hundred displayed. Even people who need to have a sale themselves drive past other jumble sales and car boot sales casting longing, lustful eyes on the beautiful piles of useless stuff set out on tables and standing up against the garage wall, watching, wondering what they could take home. The junk drive is real, it's in the blood of all of us (yes, even the Mr Neats and Ms Tidies of the world).

Clutter accumulation

Clutter begets clutter. One acquisition leads to another. Soon you're buried under generations of clobber. Yet most psychologists and professional cleaners too would agree that the desire to accumulate is brought about more by training and conditioning than by the junk fever in our veins. Let's see how this happens.

We start early, repeating the lesson over and over again so children understand 'the real value' of objects. We bribe small children to be good on boring shopping excursions by promising to buy them a toy at the toy shop. We promise children *more* toys if they'll keep the ones they've got tidily in the toy-box.

We train them to expect more donations of useless gifts on every occasion — 'Be good for Mummy, and Daddy will bring you back something nice from Bahrain.' 'What are you going to ask Father Christmas to bring you?'

Children learn that few occasions can pass in our lives without an exchange of something tangible — called a 'present'. We tell them how to save, keep, collect and store all the objects they receive, but seldom what to do with them or why they have them.

At junior school every piece of work a child does is carefully preserved — and most of it is sent home at the end of term.

When a child reaches its teens, vanity and glamour are overwhelmingly established as more important than practicality or reason — 'Now you're twelve you can have your ears pierced; have your own television set in your bedroom; experiment with make-up.'

Young people are taught to leap on bargains and to acquire 'two for the price of one' without first asking themselves if they need even one.

Serious clutter collecting often begins when we get married or buy a house. We're short of cash so parents, grandparents and aunts give us their old

17

stuff and we become so attached to it by the time we can afford better that we keep it out of sentimentality.

At last, on top of all the hoarded stuff and the new stuff, we inherit other people's life-time accumulation of possessions, and keep that too in memory of the old folks and our own childhood.

So not only do we positively *create* junk but we also allow junk to happen to us — and we do not resist.

It's helpful to understand where clutter came from, but it's a lot more important to know where it's going. . .

Don't let clutter make a monkey out of you

We've all heard the story of monkey traps. When hunters discovered how greedy and possessive monkeys are, they took coconuts, made a hole in each of them, tied them to a tree and went home. The next morning they'd return to find dozens of wild monkeys, unharmed, with their little hands stuck in the coconuts. How did this work? Simple: the hole in the coconut was cut just big enough for a monkey's hand to squeeze through; inside the coconut were placed some tasty goodies. The monkeys would creep up on the trap, smell the bait, reach in and grab a fistful of whatever — and when they tried to bring their hands out, their fists of course wouldn't pass through the hole. Unwilling to release the bait, the monkeys were caught.

Now being clever humans, we instantly reason: 'Why didn't the stupid monkeys let go of the stuff, pull their hands out, and run away?' Well, they didn't because they are, in that respect, human. They refused to let go of something they had. To hang on meant the stewpot, but the thrill of possession overruled all risk and reason.

All of us have set our hearts on things and even though they have tied us down and drained our resources, we hang on,

refusing to let go and run away to better, safer things. Our minds, like the monkeys' fists, close up and there's no giving up. Like the monkeys, we jump and scream to be free to get on with the things we want to do but we can't because we're shackled by all the belongings we refuse to let go of.

In our greed and possessiveness we hang on, even at the peril of our physical and spiritual lives.

I've seen good farmers who refused to let go of horse machinery lose everything. I've seen families refuse to sell and move out of a beloved but unproductive old farm — and deteriorate into poverty. I've watched tradesmen who hung onto old styles and procedures be forced out of business. I've watched older people miss trips and other wonderful experiences because they wouldn't release their death grip on their junk. I know people who hang onto old lost loves so tightly that no new love can squeeze in, and they wilt and die miserably. Our refusal to surrender worthless harmful worn-out things stops us growing and maturing.

We actually have to reach the point where our clutter inflicts pain or inconvenience on our physical and emotional selves before we're clever enough to think of getting rid of it. Most of the time it just lies there, dormant and useless and often out of sight — until one day we have to move it for the carpet layer, or we move to another house, or we stumble over it, or somebody makes us account for or insure it — before we consider clearing it out. It has to affect our appearance, our strength, our speed, finally offend our *vanity* enough for us to realize it would be wise to let it go. *Hanging on will hang you.*

Let's face it — there is a wisdom in letting go of things that clutter and choke your life. There is nothing more stimulating and noble than change and growth. Most of us never taste the new, the fresh; the zestful because we have our heads and hearts enslaved by clutter.

Chapter 3

A hundred and one feeble excuses for hanging on to clutter

Clutter piles up on us and chokes our lives but we are expert at devising all manner of excuses to justify keeping it. If these excuses are repeated in a reverent enough tone, no one will question them.

'But I may need it for a project'

Tons of clutter can trace its ancestry to a worthwhile enterprise. The excuse for keeping it is: I'm saving it for a Scout/school/hobby/class project. This might have been true ten years or even ten months ago, but if an undertaking is dead — by which I mean it has ceased to be either interesting or valuable because the right moment has passed, or you've moved on, or you no longer have the same set of friends and interests — *don't keep it,* even if it has cash value. Give it away or sell it before it drains all the energy it once gave you. *Decide! The unresolved is probably unnecessary.*

'But Grandad gave it to me'

Objects you'd never choose yourself, given as gifts, are a difficulty. You'd have to be a heartless wretch to throw out any gift. But do you have to keep it and put it on display?

See Chapter 7 for some guidance on this sticky subject. Ask yourself why someone gave you a gift in the first place. As a *token* of feeling and appreciation. Love isn't a tangible thing, so whether you keep the gift or not it has no effect on that all-important relationship between you and the giver. Many of those of us who keep junk gifts are insecure or egotistical — we have to keep and display the 'evidence' to assure ourselves that we're loved.

'It'll do for second best'

Is second-best clutter or a good standby? List all your second-bests and say what you're doing with them now. Suppose you've just bought a new watch, working boots, briefcase, gloves, blender, fishing rod, tennis racket, kitchen knife, kettle, sewing machine, bike, salad bowl. Where are the old ones?

Why did you obtain a new one? That's easy: because you were unhappy with the old one — it was worn out, old, getting ugly, not working right any more or you were simply tired of it. Why do we keep things we're not happy with? There's no answer, except that we're clutter collectors. Sure, there's some glimmer of hope for those old worn out watches, stiff working boots, leaky air mattresses, the bike with the bent frame, the too-small briefcase, that battered and shabby purse, that balding dress coat, the blunt knife with the cracked handle — but once you have the new one in your hand, those second-bests have lost their attraction. Don't keep them around to mess up your life!

Here's an example: everyone I know has a suitcase with a broken catch. After it pops open on the airport carousel or in the coach, they're shamed into the purchase of a nice new 'best' one. But the old one is never thrown away; it's a 'spare' or 'extra' one that, to justify its retired status, is filled with bits and pieces and stored.

'It may come in handy one day'

You may be right, *if you can find it.*

A few spare buttons is wisdom; a few jars full is ridiculous junk you'll spend hours sorting through (once you find the jars).

Most people can't find or forget where they put something when they do 'need it one day' — so they usually end up buying another one.

Another version of this old favourite is: 'I'll always be ready for———. ' The only thing clutter collectors are always ready for is a good rummage. People free of unnecessary 'stuff' are really the only ones who are prepared for action.

'This——— is still perfectly good'
'I'm saving it for spare parts'

Ever notice that when someone throws out an old shoe, the leather uppers are still in almost as good condition as when the shoe was new? Nobody has trouble throwing out the shoe, but everyone takes out the old lace and keeps it forever. I've hardly met anyone who doesn't do that, and I've never met anyone who ever uses the lace!

If there's anything resembling a good part on something worn or broken, we want to strip it off and save it, whether we need it or not: buttons, buckles, belts, the feathers and bands from old hats, doorknobs, lampshades that will never look good on another lamp, any old wheel or tyre.

Watch it, or stripped or rescued junk will overwhelm you. If you're honest with yourself, you'll realize you don't have room to keep it or time to make an inventory of it.

'As soon as I get rid of it, I'll need it'

This is one of the feeblest of all feeble excuses. The truth is, the day after we get rid of it the guilt of feeling as though we murdered it mounts up, so for the next two years we unconsciously search for a use for it and always find some weak application to feed the feeling that we disposed of it prematurely.

If we kept it, *we wouldn't use it anyway.* Only the fact that it's gone gives us the courage to think we would have.

'It's proof'

Dumping our obvious, garish, worthless junk is easy, but once, when I was having a clear out, I found undumped, on the second time round:

1. Three boxes of original edited manuscript and rough layout from my first published book.
2. A drawerful of worn-out working gloves.

3. My first wristwatch I bought in 1949.
4. My college textbooks.

None of this stuff was of any use to me — and certainly not to anyone else, so why did I keep it? For *evidence*. Because it seems that nothing can beat hard cold evidence as a souvenir of our maiden voyages through life.

Tangible objects *prove that I was there*: that I once wrote a book, that I once put up a building, that I went to college.

'But they aren't making them any more'

This may indeed be a true statement but why do you suppose they stopped making all these things in the first place? Simple — they were out of date, out of fashion or something else more efficient had replaced them.

'It's been in the family for years'

Stored in remote corners of buildings you'll find, under the dust and cobwebs, cast iron wood-burning stoves, retired mangles, old treadle sewing machines, solid iron frying pans, ghastly huge (and warped) pieces of furniture, massive electric fires, grandfather clocks with chimes so loud you can only turn them on for exhibition, etc. Their era is gone; they've been replaced by lighter, quicker, safer things — but because they're thick, heavy and have put in service time we keep and coddle them. I love these old things, and marvel at the sentiment they can stir, but we can't keep the whole house full. If we keep too many of them for 'atmosphere', we won't be able to breathe.

Who wants to lug a seventy pound hinged wooden trunk through airports when a five-pound, non-sagging fibreglass suitcase will do the job better? Sturdiness alone is not a reason to keep the

old; if so we would still use covered wagons, wooden shoes and serge stockings. If you're unwilling to *use* something, if you hardly ever *look* at it, if it doesn't delight your soul or stir memories every time you look at it, if it's just rotting out in the shed — do it (and yourself) justice by getting rid of it.

'It may be worth something some day'

The glittering illusion of the possibility that one day you might be able to sell that piece of junk for a phenomenal sum creates an excuse to cling to even the most worthless items. All sorts of appetite-whetting success stories appear in the media, telling how some lucky soul wandered into his attic and found a rare old coin, vase or painting that made him rich. But don't let them raise false hopes — only a few pieces of junk in tens of thousands are rare and valuable and if you averaged the value of all the hours spent to sort and clean it up to sell it, your wages would probably be about 5p an hour. There isn't much cash in your cupboard, mostly clutter. I've seen many people spend £50 on petrol, signs and advertising for a garage sale to take in £25 — and that isn't profitable either in terms of the wallet or of your life's time taken.

If you have doubts in your bouts of deciding what to keep, don't waste time listening to fellow hoarders. Take a few minutes and call an expert and ask, 'How much is a 1917 clothes mangle worth?' He'll know instantly — and then you can make a decision to keep or sell. Many a clutter keeper has gone to a lot of trouble to keep worthless stuff because he 'imagined' its worth. Remember, since the onset of mass production and the craze for antiques, fewer and fewer items are scarce enough to become valuable.

'I was raised during the Depression and we were taught to save everything...'

We've all heard this one and I've saved it till now because it's a real heartbreaker. It would be downright reckless to stop saving for hard times — or would it?

Horror stories of the Thirties Depression have planted fear in all of us and if such a dire event should roll around again, we want to be prepared in some way. Hair-raising stories from our parents and grandparents of no food, fuel, tools, toys or blankets give us a compassionate view of all of the clutter they're stashing away. Believe it or not, there are lots of 'depression savers' who survived the last one and are saving *everything* — rewearable, restorable, reusable or not — to have on hand during a possible future downward trend.

There is good news and bad news for you depression savers.

The good news is that your junk *will* have a use during the next depression — as fuel for your fire to keep you warm. The bad news is that the one-time thing of value will be junk. No one will have cash to buy your clutter except the filthy rich, who will already have too much of their own stuff to look after. Stow away food, friends, talent — those might save you. When things get tough, the less you have to guard, store, keep warm and carry around the better off you'll be.

We've heard ourselves and others spout these rationalizations so long that we think they're sacred. But they're not; this is why I've taken the time to assemble some of the most common of the thousands of excuses I've collected from junkees over the years.

Breeze through this condensed list of invalid excuses — excuses you'll not be allowed to use when you begin to get the clutter out of your life.

Let's start with a few of the classics:

Bent rolls of leftover Christmas wrapping paper: *'I can always iron it.'*

Correspondence and birthday cards from old acquaintances you scarcely knew even then: *'I need to copy these addresses off the envelopes.'*

Abandoned do-it-yourself projects you found you couldn't do yourself: *'I'm going to write to the company and tell them their instructions are lousy.'*

Dresses and trousers you haven't been able to zip up for years: *'They're a good incentive to lose weight.'*

Three-quarters-full notebooks from evening classes: *'I may want to brush up on that one day.'*

Saucepans and buckets that leak: *'These might be nice outside somewhere with petunias planted in them.'*

Faded bedspreads and curtains from former homes: *'Maybe I could dye them.'*

Stacks of loo roll, aluminium foil and clingwrap centres: *'I'm saving these for when I have grandchildren.'*

Never-used gadgets and fancy attachments for now-defunct equipment: *'This is still a perfectly good automatic toenail polisher.'*

Tights with a two-inch ladder up one leg: *'I can always wear them with trousers.'*

Long outdated packets of garden seeds: *'Those expiration dates are just gimmicks to get you to buy new seeds.'*

The mini dresses you used to wear with thigh boots: *'I can always convert these to tunics.'*

Lone earring: *'I can always make it into a pendant.'*

Pots from all the plants that died: *'If I have no bits and pieces at all I'll be too sterile a person.'*

Fabric scraps your mother, sisters, cousins and friends were delighted to get rid of: *'I'm a natural scavenger.'*

The stained and sagging couch that's perfect for the family room you don't have: *'I'm saving this in case I have to furnish another house.'*

Stacks of Christmas cards you got in previous years: *'I'm going to take up collage when I retire.'*

Half-finished sewing project that you ended up hating: *'Maybe when my daughter gets this size she'll finish it.'*

Sound familiar?

A cruel fact of clutter is that there is no one to blame — it is mostly *our* fault. Yet we often feel abused — the 'world' (our parents, our mate, the government, the company, our society) has inflicted it on us, we were innocent bystanders, seduced and left wounded.

My favourite wall motto:

"Your situation is exactly what you make it, or what you allow it to be."

No one guides your quivering hand in a junk shop but you, no one holds your face in junk reading, viewing and listening, no one but you says yes or no, keep it or throw it. Your present clutter quotient is where *you* put it, where *you* allow it to be. None of the excuses listed in this chapter (or any new ones you might think up) can excuse clutter or the damage it will do.

24

Chapter 4

Junkosis

Junkosis is a slow, painful strangulation and dying of the senses. Although our brains are still intact, we've simply replaced *thinking* with *things*. We've crowded out creativity with accumulation. We've frozen flexibility with profusion. We've snapped up so much free stuff and bought so many things to keep, store, clean, polish and protect that we don't have any freedom.

Junkees are destined to succumb to junkosis. They are the ones with a tendency to load up plates, places, vaults, homes and conversations with more than is needed.

Junkees are afflicted with the endless urge to have more. Enough is never enough. Have you ever wondered why most frauds, schemes, cons, embezzlements, etc., aren't committed by the desperately hard up but by the nice well-to-do citizen? People with plenty, position and more things than they can already use are often the people who defraud to get more. Prisons are filled with

people who never could get enough.

Junk is insidious because its accummulation is so gradual. Like those extra pounds of flesh, it silently, sneakily mounts up and around, on top of and under us until we're surrounded. It's all so slow and subtle we don't realize how much of it there is.

Clutter Will Cramp Your Style

In 1979 I took ten Boy Scouts on a two-week camping trip. We were to spend eleven days on foot with a pack, hiking from camp to camp. We were cautioned before we started out about footwear, weather conditions, getting lost, etc. Then, sensing our junkee tendencies, the ranger put us through a kit inspection. We had to spread a blanket in front of our tent and empty our packs out on it, showing everything we were going to take on the eleven-day hike. (It shamefully revealed everything from toothpicks to love notes.) Then the ranger walked around and picked out everyone's treasures, giving reasons such as, 'You won't use this,' 'This is silly,' 'This is too heavy,' 'This attracts wasps.' Out went the smuggled radios, bulky binoculars, hair dryers, cast iron kettles, comics and all that was junk on the hike. The ranger said, 'We have a tendency on our journeys to take more than we want to end up carrying.' I nodded agreement and saw to it that my boys had lighter loads. Then I spotted the fold-up fishing rod and other things the ranger had booted out of *my* pile of goodies. I repacked my rucksack, and, when the ranger wasn't looking, threw in some books (a taboo), a couple of sharpening stones, two wood rasps and a few other extras in case I had some spare time. This made my pack a firm, compact fifty-five pounds. For ten days and nights in temperatures ranging from 5° to 25°C, going up and down 10,000-foot peaks, fording slippery streams, I sagged under my pack and stumbled over my dragging feet, groaning, promising myself that never again would I take more than I could carry. My unnecessary extras were such a burden I could scarcely enjoy the fun of the trip.

Clutter is doing the same thing to your journey through life — your job, bringing up your family, going to school. Unnecessary possessions will dilute the quality of our life, not add to it as we thought when we packed them in.

As a means of demobilizing people, clutter rates with crippling diseases, being bedridden, unable to drive or trapped in a prison cell. The things we don't need tie us down — keep us away from adventure, affection and accomplishment — and we can't go when and where we want to.

Clutter seldom gets the blame for life's problems, but it's one of the biggest contributors (if not *the* biggest). There is probably more violence, more arguments, fights and killings over worthless junk than over anything else.

Marriage and family failures are often the result of having too many possessions. Often couples have so insulated themselves with clutter in the form of excess clothing, jewellery, hobby gear, gadgets, vehicles, etc., that they can't get to each other to love. When we're extending our feelings to inanimate objects, we're exhausting emotions that could be generating affection. When loving people come our way they can't find us or our feelings. And this dulling of our sensitivity and compassion by junk and clutter is so gradual that few of us realize it's happening.

There's no escape from the toll clutter takes of our life. The most valuable 'come-in-handy-one-day' junk will obstruct our emotional freedom if we let it pile up on us. Everything stashed away or hidden, discreetly or indiscreetly, is also stashed away in our mind and is draining our mental energy. We can't hide our rubbish in a deep enough hole or in obscure enough corners to keep it out of our mind. Once physically discarded, it's also discarded from our mind, and we're free from keeping mental tabs on it. But as long as we own it, we'll mentally tend it. We feel obliged to use our junk, whether we need it or not. If we don't or can't use it, then we worry about why we have it at all! Junk will get you — don't sit there and argue that it won't.

The guilt of junk possession is overwhelming. Just get someone talking about their junk and stand back and listen: it's like a public confession of sin. Feeling guilty and frustrated about our piles of clutter, knowing we have to deal with the problem but not knowing where to start — or really wanting to — is prejunkosis depression. Watch out!

Junkosis is generally the real culprit when people cave in or fall apart in despair and discouragement. Useless possessions push our thoughts, time, budget, space and physical energies to the edge. Then, when the *real* crises of death, sadness or separation come along, we haven't the capacity to cope with them. We just don't have anything left to give: we've burned so much fuel preserving our junk that we have little or none to burn the torch of strength when it's needed. A big strain on an already strained capacity usually results in failure, if not disaster. But demand on a person who isn't worrying about clutter just causes him or her to work harder and get through the crisis.

I had a mild case of junkosis, as most of us do. How can *you* tell if you're a likely victim of this disease?

If you wander through shops and go to car boot sales when you don't need anything in particular, you're infected.

Signs of Junkosis

The sure sign of evolution from a mild to a chronic junkee is when we save (or even have the *urge* to save) disposables. Many things are made just well enough to be used once, then discarded. With great imagination or dexterity they might serve another turn but all in all a disposable thing, for the sake of health and wealth, should be disposed of.

Before you think of pointing the finger at all your friends who are saving no-return bottles, examine your own behaviour.

Are you:
- saving lids from old jars?

- little plastic hangers from new pairs of socks?
- keeping plastic bags?
- tempted to reuse a tea bag?
- promoting 'throwaway' plastic cups to the china cupboard?
- keeping and using foil pie tins until they're wrinkled beyond recognition?
- slow to throw away blunt disposable razors?
- saving Chinese take-away containers?
- hoarding those sweet little film canisters?
- saving the boxes from every piece of jewellery you've every bought or been given?
- keeping the packaging from domestic appliances (in case you move)?
- stockpiling empty pill bottles?
- stuffing bits of food in the freezer because you can't decide what to do with them?
- keeping old keys that don't open anything.

If you answered 'yes' to three or more, keep reading.

Junk Shows on You

No matter how sharp you are, what you own, how famous you are — if you eat, wear, live and love junk it will cause ugly bulges somewhere on your person or in your character.

A junkee works more and more hours to get more money to spend on excess, things he doesn't need, that he never has or takes the time to enjoy. We run in this circle of watching, chasing and weighing junk until we drop — or just wear out.

Junkees gain little sympathy from friends or loved ones. People feel compassion for the sick or handicapped, but where sickness is self-induced (cirrhosis of the liver, insomnia) and is essentially self-abuse, people feel that somehow we got what we deserved.

We've become so conditioned to clutter's call that we care more for 'things' than we do for *our own lives*. Once, years ago, native American and white men were working on a big reservoir construction project, when the levee gate broke and a flash flood descended on the workers. Although all the workers were together in the same area, when the casualty report was finished, all the twenty-five white workers had drowned — and not one of the Indians. How could that happen?

One of the Indians had the answer: 'When the dam broke and the big water came, we Indians saw, we ran for our lives, we reached high ground. The white man ran for his money, and he drowned.

Why wait until clutter has choked you to death before thrusting it off?

Chapter 5

The economy of clutter

The well-known eighty/twenty rule of business says: If all of a given category of items is sorted in order of value, eighty per cent of the value will come from only twenty per cent of the items. Think about that in terms of clutter. Eighty per cent of the space on our shelves (and in our minds) is occupied by stuff we never need.

Eighty per cent of our family fun comes from twenty per cent of the games and equipment and puzzles we've got jammed into our cupboards. (How much of the remaining eighty per cent could be thrown away without it ever being missed?) Eighty per cent of our reading enjoyment and information comes from twenty per cent of the material in our bookcases and magazine racks. (How much of the unopened eighty per cent would we ever miss?) Eighty per cent of our home maintenance and upkeep is done with twenty per cent of the accumulated paraphernalia in our cellars and garages. (How much of the remaining eighty per cent is unnecessary clutter?) Eighty per cent of the outfits we wear come from twenty per cent of the clothes cramming our cupboards and drawers. (How much of the remaining eighty per cent could Oxfam get more use from than we do?) Is this all just fancy business theory? Not on your life! If you got rid of the eighty per cent that's clutter you'd be more than twenty per cent more efficient.

Clutter makes every job take longer

Clutter is one of the greatest enemies of efficiency and stealers of time — and that includes yours.

For every chore he tackles, the average person spends more time getting ready — looking for a place, the tools, a reason to do it, etc. — than actually doing it. It takes only six seconds to drive a nail in, often ten minutes to find the nails and hammer. But the nailing is all that counts and brings the benefit; the fumbling and searching don't. If the tools for a job are buried in mountains of paraphernalia we never get started — we just thrash around.

Clutter makes every job harder and makes cleaning take forever. Any project we tackle, from building to disassembling, will be slowed down, dampened and diluted if we constantly have to fight our way to it in the midst of clutter. As a professional carpet cleaner, I noticed that sometimes my crew would clean a large living room in one hour; sometimes exactly the same size room and type of carpet took three or four hours. First I thought some workers were just plain slower than others — but closer scrutiny proved I was wrong. In the first house, for example, it took fifteen minutes to move stuff, forty-five to shampoo, and fifteen to move the stuff back; in the second it took one and a half hours to move stuff, forty-five minutes to shampoo, and one and a half hours to move the stuff back. There was so much stuff you could barely find the floors.

If things you don't use are taking up good storage space it means you have to reach further and dig deeper to get the tool, book, suitcase, shirt, etc., you need. 'Getting something out', instead of being a few-seconds job, often ends up a twenty-minute search-and-rescue mission.

Take the crowded shelves of the average kitchen cupboard. You're making soup one day and decide to throw in a tin of tomatoes. You have to rummage past the celery soup bought by mistake, the canned lotus root for the Indian dinner you've never got around to preparing, the aged butter beans you ought to throw away, and the rum extract you use only at Christmas. You find a tin of tomatoes and tip them into the soup — whoops, they're the elegant plum tomatoes you were saving for a sauce, not the ordinary old ones you wanted, but they're tomatoes. Later, putting the left-over soup away, you rummage through the odd containers, that incredible assortment of glass jars you've saved and all that Tupperware, and finally find a plastic margarine pot that's just the right size. But where's the lid? You try lid after lid from the pile. None fit. You push the containers aside on the shelf thinking the lid must have rolled to the back — and you knock over a jar, which falls on the floor, shattering and spraying shrapnel over half the kitchen. You now have to sweep or vacuum the whole kitchen and completely empty the bottom of the cupboard (the toolbox, the garden sprayer, those flattened slippers and bags of rags, the fan heater, the cat litter) to make sure you've eliminated all those deadly splinters of glass.

The junk in your cupboard has just cost you an extra half an hour in one day. An unnecessary half hour of shuffling clutter around every day adds up to an entire week each year. (And how many of us repeat this sad scenario in one form or another *more* than once a day?)

Clutter in interior design

As a consultant for interior design, I've become extra-conscious of the tendency to clutter up even construction. We seem to take quality items (even beautiful, expensive building materials), then pile, I mean almost *cram*, them on to a structure — trying to give it life or looks or 'atmosphere'. While sitting in a lecture hall of a fine university, I noted that in the decor of that one room there were nine different types of material making up the walls: glass, wood panelling, carpet, stainless steel, tile, paint, fabric wall covering, brick facing and Formica — all fine materials. But to maintain all the variations in surface material and texture

took an extra cleaner and cleaning trolley the size of a car (which made marks on the floor as it moved around). Whenever we try to crowd in too much, we pay a toll in maintenance — and the end result is less time for living.

This goes back to the first value of de-junking: it creates simplicity. The amount of time saved by simplicity is phenomenal.

Don't let clutter erode your leisure time

Have you noticed that as we grow older we have less time to do things? At the age of ten we had all day to play, make something or get a chore done; at eighteen, only part of the day; then, years later, we often have only minutes. We simply have so many more people, places, and things crowded into our lives that we *have* to become more efficient if we intend to make good use of the little spare time we have.

I found this the case with my music. Recently I had fifteen minutes free to play one or two pieces, and attacked my music

pile — it took ten minutes of sorting and digging to find the music I wanted, so I ended up with only five minutes to play. I suddenly realized that ninety per cent of my pile of music was never used — and it was actually stopping me enjoying the ten per cent of it I loved.

The day I decided to sort out my music was the day I began to have time to use and enjoy it again. What a change — no more sorting and searching and rummaging — I use *all* the time now just to play.

The value is in the using

Rich people, poor people — when it comes to junk, one is as bad as the other; one's junk may just be a little more expensive. Rich people are notorious collectors of things they always wanted when they were growing up. There are people who all their lives dream about the country cottage or restaurant or yacht or whatever they want above all, and as their life nears its end they finally accumulate the cash to make the dream come true. Even if they can't use it much, they go and

32

buy it — thinking that having it is the ultimate thing. But it all comes to little because they can't smell and feel and share in the glory of production. The value is in the using and building and growing, not simply the *having*. They have to pay someone else to look after it for them; they only get the woes and financial drain; maybe once a year they visit it and look over their kingdom — it generally becomes just another possession to them.

Even those of us whose acquisition is on a small scale should ask: how often do you have to use something to justify owning it? Don't be overawed by ownership. 'I own it' is a ridiculous statement to make about anything, when you think about it. *Use* is the only value a thing has. War, fire, flood, famine, robbery or death can end ownership instantly. Don't get too attached to 'mine' — *my land, my house, my boat, my car, my golf clubs*. . . might be my undoing.

Like you, I hate to rent, I'd rather not borrow, I like to own — but don't be too proud to change. People buy £500 worth of ski stuff to ski once a year, or a 30-foot ladder to reach the eaves of the house once every four or five years. In either case they could hire the right equipment and not only save money but the lugging, storing, selecting, insuring, and general complication of their lives. *Use* should be the deciding factor — and not just *will*, but *how often* will you use it. And do you really like (or need) what it will do for you? Maybe you could just eliminate the activity or purpose it's 'needed' for from your life.

Storing it costs

Out of sight, out of mind might apply to lovers, but not to junk. We pay money and emotion for it, no matter where it is.

Storage space — (or, more specifically, lack of it) is one of the most frequently asked questions in the 'house care' world. There never seems to be enough. It never crosses our minds that it's what we have too much of — not too little of — that causes the problem.

Not only is up to twenty-five per cent of our homes devoted to storage, but we have to find ways and means beyond our own walls to store the overflow. And once we discover how easy it is to damage something by packing it too tightly or packing a heavy item on top of it, we take the reverse approach and pack inefficiently, wasting the space we do have. But no matter *how* we store, we expand. We stuff it under beds, under stairs, in wall units, in attics, basements, boiler rooms, 'spare' rooms, we fill the garage and the garage roof space with it, then migrate to the garden and get little sheds. . . they are filled up and then we try to find a garage to rent for more storage.

Why do people store things in another place? Because *they aren't using them!*

A rented storage unit is a kind of oversized Emotional Withdrawal box (see Chapter 16).

The things we keep served us well and enriched our lives — but when that time of our life is past, we should get rid of the old junk so we can have the freedom to greet a new season and grow again. Paying ransom in money, time or emotion for bygone clutter is pathetic.

Remember!

Storage costs money; serves as an enticement to theft; makes excellent fuel for house fires.

Protecting it costs

If your junk is valuable enough for you to be willing to take the time to move it and the money to store it, it may also be attractive to predators — both the two-legged and six-legged variety. And then you have to protect it.

You can either take the fortress approach — Banham locks, an intruder-eating Doberman and an expensive sophisticated alarm system — or store your smaller valuables in those costly and inconvenient little safe-deposit boxes — or cold storage. No matter how you choose to guard the mink, the emeralds, the home computer, or your super-good sound system, it takes time, money and mental effort. And of course, it all has to be insured.

Insurance is simple, you say? Just pay the premium. However, other 'premiums' are paid, in the case, for example, of elaborate alarm systems. I've been in homes where the anti-burglar devices are so complicated it's hard for the owner even to get out without hassle (let's not even discuss the complexities of getting in). And every night the alarms have to be set, just before the four hours of sleep you might get before the police roust you out to investigate the false alarm.

Only you can decide whether it's worth having to de-mothball and re-mothball your fur opera cape every time you wear it, or to remember to switch off the car's burglar alarm so that a policeman doesn't come at you with handcuffs, or to pick up your great-aunt Edna's silver from the bank every Christmas and take it back afterwards. But you at least ought to *think* about whether it's worth it — instead of automatically going to all that trouble.

Moving it costs

The average family might move six or seven times in a lifetime. If a third of your stuff is clutter, you could save four removal van loads if you de-junked! People spend literally millions moving things they don't need.

We all haul junk around at great expense and effort when we move house, not to mention all that moving of things from room to room, to and from all our storage areas, in our briefcases and even in our pockets!

It's an unnecessary load; get rid of it before you move — it's a lot easier to cope with *before* than after. You'll *never* have the time to 'sort through it'. If you have any hint you're going to move, de-junk three months before and you'll bless yourself for it.

Tragedy ... clutter's ultimate cost

Far too many cheerful, playing children smother to death each year in carelessly discarded fridges and containers; many die painfully from old poisons and cleaners thrown in tips and even left illegally in ditches and on waste ground; hundreds die in fires caused by carelessly stored solvents and fuels, or from negligent smoking habits. Junk!

Many an adult is laid low by clutter in the home. Notice how often the accident results from some kind of junk we were too lazy or too sentimental to get rid of.

Many a car accident happens because of objects in cars that impede or distract the driver. Junk! If clutter doesn't inflict some physical damage on you, it'll take its toll on you mentally — you can count on it.

Age – don't fight it

If the old alchemists had truly found a fountain of youth, many of us would enthusiastically immerse some of our clutter before ourselves. Ageing is a natural life process in ourselves *and* in the things we use — accept it! We mess up our quality of life by trying to retard ageing, cosmetically or otherwise. When an era, an item, a car, a system grows old, let it go. We can't stop ageing, but we can start new things and grow and enjoy again instead of letting dying junk take some of our strength with it.

We've been taught we're bad if we waste — 'waste not, want not.' But we waste more valuable time and energy doing up and trying to save worthless junk than many an object was ever worth originally.

Like you, I'd never think of throwing away anything I like that's still good. But why not be a little more realistic about the things which are almost done for? We often foolishly risk our financial (and physical) necks trying to squeeze five per cent more use out of an item that has served its honourable time.

'I'll mend it!'

About two per cent of broken junk is ever mended. Mass-produced moulded or stamped objects of this era are difficult to repair. (Forget the miracle glue advertisements, because few things will stick together as permanently as your fingers.) Few people have the time or facilities to mend things, and most of us don't like to use or display patched stuff anyway. Do you or your kids wear patched clothes? Rarely! Do you know how many heels broken off high-heeled shoes are waiting somewhere to be fixed? Well, they can't, and won't be.

Most things wear out first, then break or cease to operate — but a few things *do* break while they are in the prime of life, and it's uneconomical to 'bury' them. They can and should be mended, and the act of fixing them can contribute triumphantly to your emotional well-being.

'MEND-IT' TALLY SHEET

Answer honestly – how many of these broken items have you mended lately?

- ☐ shredded cassette tapes
- ☐ hair dryer/hot combs
- ☐ saucepan handles
- ☐ broken chairs
- ☐ torn upholstery
- ☐ toasters or toasted sandwich makers that burn
- ☐ leaky teapots
- ☐ Christmas tree lights that don't
- ☐ chaise longues with rotted webbing
- ☐ dead torches
- ☐ loose-headed hammers
- ☐ defective clocks/watches
- ☐ inaccurate thermometers
- ☐ broken pushchairs
- ☐ socks or sweaters with a hole in them
- ☐ umbrellas with one cracked rib
- ☐ broken scissors
- ☐ sagging venetian blinds
- ☐ shaky card tables
- ☐ broken electrical cords
- ☐ seized-up lawn mowers
- ☐ TV with a wonky tube
- ☐ specs with broken frames
- ☐ broken mobiles
- ☐ dismantled lamps
- ☐ chipped teacups
- ☐ broken aerials
- ☐ broken zips
- ☐ dismembered dolls
- ☐ injured musical instruments
- ☐ cracked dishes
- ☐ unstrung rackets
- ☐ suitcases that won't do up
- ☐ wobbly chair legs/arms

15-34   You must own a repair shop.
10-15   You must be tight fisted.
5-10   Your TV must be broken.
2-5   You deserve applause.
0-1   You're normal (and honest).

Now get rid of the ones you haven't mended and sigh a great sigh of relief.

It's amazing how we forge a relationship with a thing; we actually think we owe it something — surgery, even a life-support system if necessary.

We don't owe it anything. It probably isn't worth mending so don't let love affairs with things clutter up your life. They have a way of worming their way into your heart, but be objective: if it isn't worth mending, throw it away (without a wake or mourning).

Twelve hands are better than two

The picking up of *other* people's belongings is the most inefficient and expensive clutter cost of all — like the mother who spends all her time picking up after an untidy husband and careless children. Women all over the world are wasting their youth and high spirits and creativity playing caretaker to their families. If your family habitually leaves clutter around they're going to keep doing it — are you going to keep picking it up? Do you think tolerating that kind of thoughtlessness in them is really doing them a favour? Have a family meeting and tell everyone over two years old that mess must be picked up/cleaned up by whoever makes it. They'll be better people for it!

Littering

The litter lout is an inconsiderate clutter-strewer who thinks nothing of harming his fellow humans or the environment.

In many buildings more is spent on cleaning up and providing bins for cigarette ends, can rings, crisp packets, chewing gum, etc. in the entrance hall and outside than on maintaining all of the paths, lawns and flower beds. *Clutter – our own or other peoples – doesn't come cheap in our lives; we pay for it.* I don't want to be guilty of foisting my junk on others, do you?

Any residue we leave in life should be contained. If we are old enough to make a mess, we are old enough to clear up after ourselves.

Chapter 6

Home sweet home...
full of junk!

Do you need a double garage... maybe a triple?... or do you need a commitment to de-clutter?

While cleaning a large, plush home during my first year at college, I managed to wade through and clean a luxurious, treasure-laden bedroom and embarked on cleaning the clothes cupboard. In addition to the expected arsenal of pricey wearing apparel, I had to move five exquisite cigarette lighters, forty-seven pairs of women's shoes (I kid you not), a case of 1920s *National Geographic Magazines* several tennis racquets, fourteen boxes of Christmas cards, a side-saddle, six poodle collars, and numerous other items. It was a tidy but completely full cupboard, in harmony with the style of the woman who lived there. She was fifty-five years old, and possessed a handsome home filled with elaborate art and delicate tapestries, carved furniture and exotic lamps that she had spent part of her life collecting and the rest of her life cleaning and dusting and keeping track of. This project of shuffling treasures around had taken her over half a lifetime; she had been amassing clutter for thirty-five years.

Does that sound a little like someone you know? How about this story? Some friends of mine helped a family move into a new home. They piled all their stuff in several downstairs rooms, lived there for a while, and like most of us, never got round to sorting through all the stuff they dragged around with them. They decided to have a fireplace put in the living room downstairs and called a local builder. When they gave him the address he thought for a minute and said, 'I put a fireplace in there two years ago.' They ran downstairs, moved the junk, and there it was — a fireplace!

Another friend told me his mother was a 'collector'. Since her health was no longer robust, she had to move from her home of fifty years to a flat. When her son and a helper went to move her belongings (she'd told them to bother only with the good stuff) they backed a sixteen-foot-long pantechnicon up to the side of the house and started in the attic. They filled the lorry right up — and were still on the upstairs. The son, an avid junk collector himself, only managed to salvage a couple of boxes of 'good stuff' for his mum and

37

one small box for himself; the rest was pure, uadulterated clutter. The woman never missed the three lorryloads her son took to the tip, and found her de-junked life a happy one.

Most of us are in the same condition as the owner of forty-seven pairs of shoes. We can find our fireplace, but not our matches, and our junk could strain a semi instead of a pantechnicon truck. Our house treasures may not be as expensive, but we have as many cubbyholes for them — that we shuffle through, sort and re-sort, climb over, worry about and maintain for hours on end.

Not only can we not take it with us when that final departure date arrives, but keeping it with us under the same roof is creating more conflict than we imagine. We really can't win with clutter. Sooner or later we're sick of it, tired of being a slave to it. It doesn't matter if it's valuable or not: if it's unused, in the way and takes emotional and mental energy away from us, we feel guilty about it — in fact, deep in our heart, we hate it. Every time we come home from the shops with more pictures, trinkets and goodies for the walls, shelves, drawers and sideboards, we're more frustrated because there's nowhere to put anything. We're tormented by the thought that we may have to throw out something so there will be room for the new — in a house that already looks like a department store or a jumble sale. There are rarities hanging all over the place. We want to show everything off but sad to say, few people are interested in our belongings. We toil to accumulate things that will impress others, but when it comes to house junk, nice or elaborate, little kids don't care, teenagers think our obsession with inanimate objects is obscene, rich friends hate us for our cheap junk, poor friends hate us for rich junk, medium friends think we're showing off because our junk matches theirs. There is truth in all of these things — plus the fact that the house is using *us* instead of us using and enjoying *it*.

Clutter is alarming, not charming

Most junk is an overkill; that's exactly what makes it junk. I read an article in a home magazine, titled 'Put Charm in Your Bathroom.' It took a nice functional easy-to-clean bathroom and added ungodly apparatus to every surface and fixture — wall hangings, inlaid shelves, decorative cabinets, elaborate lights and accessories that made it look grotesque as well as being a nightmare to clean.

It's hard to do much living in a living room these days. There's so much stuff on the window ledges, coffee tables, bookcases and magazine racks that a rail has to be installed so none of it will fall off. Lamps are lucky to find a place to roost these days and even places to *sit* are at a premium. The floor, too, is taken up with ceramic wolfhounds, ivy-planted spittoons, and colonial cat doorstops tailor-made for tripping over. Apart from being difficult to move around in, it's hard to dust and vacuum and straighten up a cluttered living room — and that's the room we always want to have looking nice for visitors.

We do much the same thing with clothes, jewellery, food — often until the clutter almost totally obscures function, i.e., the doorlatch to the bathroom is so fancy, we can't work out how to get in.

A workshop is a place to work, relax, create, and mend things in. A kitchen is a place to conveniently cook. Look at what we have done and are doing to both these areas. Kitchens are getting so overdesigned with accessories, decorations, gadgets, and 'storage' space that we're afraid to cook in them because we'll mess them up, or they'll take too long to clean afterwards.

Every other issue of home magazines has an article on 'beautifying your kitchen': the pictures show a room rife with aspic moulds and giant stirring spoons, and displaying so many colours and textures it looks like a builder's showroom.

There are enough ovens and cooking apparatus to feed a whole barracks of soldiers. There are racks, holders, clamps and even art objects so thick on the walls and shelves that the average person would do £50 worth of damage just trying to have a bowl of cornflakes. If you have too many things at least half of them are unnecessary. Don't let those who don't *use* kitchens talk you into one of those gorgeous galleys of gimmicks and gadgets. It will only clutter and complicate your life.

A hammer, saw and bench was a workshop in the early days when we actually made things. Now we spend most of our time mounting and storing all our new progressive tools and producing nothing. Did you know the average man with a workshop buys his shelves ready-made?

Everyone of us has magpie inclinations and we express them by hoarding clutter in out of sight places (attics, cellars, cupboards, under beds, in the loft, under the stairs). Look round your house and in your private nesting areas. I bet you'll find scores of secret caches.

It's not enough to de-junk the visible eyesores — 'out of sight, out of mind' doesn't apply here. Your hidden 'magpie's nest' will clutter your mind as well as your premises.

Room spells doom

Too often we judge our capacity to own by the room we have available, not our actual need. Some homes have more than a hundred places deliberately designed to harbour junk. Now add to that the additional possibilities of a pantry, assorted knick-knack and curio shelves, various nooks and crannies, an attic and/or basement (with all the attendant boxes and trunks), a garage, a rented unit, a friend's (or relative's) spare room, and you're talking about well over a hundred and fifty places!

With over a hundred hidy-holes for junk, is it any wonder we get a headache just looking for something or when we think about cleaning cupboards or getting ready to invite guests?

The amount of room or places available in your home for 'stuff' can have either a disciplinary or a devastating effect on you. If you start thinking it's wasteful to leave space unfilled, you're lost. Walls don't have to be peppered with pictures, attics don't have to be insulated with magazines and old clothes. Basements don't have to resemble clutter-ageing cellars! Just because a shelf exists doesn't mean that is has to be filled; ripping it down or leaving it stark and simple are choices, too. Drawers are for the convenience of keeping active everyday usables out of sight and unsoiled by dust — they aren't archival vaults for junk. Space is reasonable and relaxing.

Don't put it out to grass

Many of us not only have our homes and garages filled but have junk out to pasture yet further afield. We have a boat in our brother-in-law's drive, a trailer in the shed over at Grandpa's. And the most convenient place of all (once the glory holes under our own roof are exhausted) is the parents' house!

Only a low-down cur would inflict clutter on his or her parents. When you leave home it's only moral, decent and merciful to take all your belongings with you. Parents have enough of their own; how can you put them in the position of caretakers looking after yours too? You may choose to inflict clutter on yourself for various reasons, but forcing, because of family ties, your rubbish on someone else (who feels *obliged* to store it) is unforgivable. Go and get it straightaway — they need the room!

De-junk or perish

With all that we have to worry about in our busy lives, it's not necessarily our fault that things accumulate so fast (and in so many places!). But rationalizing worthlessness after we discover it *is* our fault. Most of us will go to all kinds of lengths in order to avoid that inevitable showdown with our home junk.

But, as you know, this mad deception can only go on for so long (maybe five or ten years). Eventually we all must come to the same point — de-junk or perish!

Free yourself from household imprisonment

Freeing yourself from junk will automatically free you from housework (and it won't take any soap and water either). If you'll just de-junk your home, you'll have the time to take that course, write that book, run that marathon or make that visit.

The big question is whether it is *active* or *inactive*. Even an unsightly pile of stuff is not junk if it's stimulating some personal or group improvement.

Too much is junk... so is too nice

Something that is 'too nice to use' is undoubtedly about the most ridiculous kind of junk one can own.

Let's sit down and make a list of the things we have now that are stored, hidden, still in the box, etc. — because they're 'too good to use'. You'll be surprised how many things you have — lots of it is clutter! Use it or lose it.

Racked, stacked, packed away

One very good reason to de-clutter is to allow you to find and use all that 'good stuff' you've almost forgotten you have. You know you have it: Is it in the kitchen cupboard, or the hall cupboard, or. . . ? How embarrassing to have so much clutter you don't even remember where it all is! Having extra vacuum cleaner bags, spare fuses, candles, a cake decorating set, a chimney cleaning set, a hiking compass is no use when you can't find them. When you don't know where something is, you'll dig like a hungry dog for a bone trying to unearth it and tear up every storage area

in the whole house.

Basically, de-cluttering your home involves getting rid of the things you don't use, that you don't enjoy, that aren't necessary. This leaves plenty of room for the things you really need, because *where* you put the things that will be used is important.

Make sure you have a place to put everything you really do use that's close to where you use it.

Think about the way you live and the things you use most often; this is the stuff that should go at the front of drawers or on the most accessible shelves. Refills should be stored as near as possible to where you'll run out. Remember not to pack objects in so tightly that you can't shut the drawer again unless everything is just so; you should be able to reach into a cupboard or drawer and get a commonly used item without disarranging everything else. And while you're at it, set up a loose classification system to help you remember where things are — medicines at the top of the bathroom cabinet, for instance, toiletries at the bottom.

Converting clutter by relocating it

Some things we like and use are clutter only because of where they're located. We had some of the best fruits and fresh potatoes and carrots and all sorts of good things from our farm. However, they were in the vegetable store, fifty yards across the snow and ice from our kitchen. That fifty yards caused lots of good food to rot, because when we wanted something it meant coats, hats, boots and shovelling the snow away from the shed door. Most of the time we decided we didn't want it that badly and so didn't go. Had they been in the next room, we would have eaten and enjoyed them all.

We all have lots of good things that are not used simply because we don't keep them somewhere handy. What good is a pocket knife in the top dresser drawer? Where is your torch at this moment? I bet if the main fuse blew, a real search would begin in the dark. The torch (at least one) should be by the fuse box. Your umbrella: how many of the people you see wilting in the rain have umbrellas at home — almost all of them! Why are those people getting wet? They couldn't find an umbrella, or it was on a top shelf in an upstairs room — getting it down wasn't worth the effort. When you can't find it, can't reach it or it's not handy, what good is it? And much clutter comes from things that are so inconveniently kept you can't

be bothered to put them back.

Do me and yourself a favour. When going through your junk and all that good stuff you buy and never use, ask the big question about locations. You'll be surprised at what you can use and not have to store or throw away. I don't need to outline the exact process for you because your places and purposes are different from mine. It will be easy.

Do you really need more than one?

Owning more than one of frequently used objects such as measuring tapes may seem logical but knowing you have more than one of something around has a way of making you more careless ('I'm bound to stumble across one of them') — and all that extra clutter compounds your problems.

I struggled with this for twenty-nine years, and finally worked it out. One is easier to keep track of than eight. Then I did three things that helped:

1. Put my name on it (big!).
2. Decided on an exact place to put it.
3. Always *returned* it to that spot the minute I had finished with it

Knowing where everything is is important, but I'm the last person to direct anyone to a tidy/perfect/set way to put, hang or box everything. More and more bags, hangers, racks and boxes aren't an asset; they just help turn de-junking into re-junking — they're *junk bunkers*!

Junk bunkers

We finally reach the day when our clutter is so overwhelming that there's not a single place left to put anything: even the walls are full. It is then that we're most vulnerable to the hidden persuasion of a *junk bunker*. That, simply, is an item we can use to store more unused things in, stacked higher and packed tighter. Junk bunkers come in various models, all waiting to be piled up:

- There's that **seven-storey tool box** that encourages us to buy piles of handsome exotic hardware to fill it.
- The **solid oak knife block** with four empty slots — which leaves us no choice but to buy four more knives we don't need.
- The **desk organizer** that collects up all the bits and pieces off our desk top and holds them in an upright position.
- The **multi-pouch shoe holder** where shoes can nestle for years before they're thrown out.
- **Vinyl binders** which allow us to keep all those old magazines.
- The **new shelves** we feel compelled to fill with vases and other bric-a-brac.
- Those **two extra rooms** we built for 'just-in-case' have to be filled with furniture.

Have you ever noticed that most of the books and articles on how to organize a house more efficiently really show how to hang up, hide, file, tolerate and make decorative use of junk?

Junk bunkers are like a shot of morphine: they ease the pain, take care of the problem for a short time — and then back it comes. Most of them can accommodate only a *little* junk, and as they become overfull, they also become saggy and ugly and dangerous. They don't sort our stuff in quite the way that would be most useful, or they have too many or too few drawers for what we have/need. Or they tempt us to over-organize things in a way that isn't really

*Oh, no! It's **much** too good to look at!*

functional or realistic — so we don't keep it up. And they collect dust and are hard to clean.

If you've stooped to buying organizers, you're swinging on rusty hinges. Once you get all that junk neatly placed in or on the organizer, pick it up and chuck it out, bunker and all!

Where did all that stuff in the bunkers come from? Well, a lot of it is home gadgets.

Gadgets. . . do they make life easier?

We in the West are bombarded with clever, handy gadgets that are not really needed but are too tempting to turn down. Just because something works faster and neater than we do doesn't necessarily mean it saves time or makes life easier. It all depends on when and how often we use it, how much time and effort it takes to care for it, and how well it really does the job on hand.

High on the list of useless gadgets/tools is the bargain store do-it-yourself spray gun. The bait for suckers on this gadget is, 'Just press a button (or pull a trigger) and hey presto, the work is done.' But they don't work half the time (they clog so easily), they're tricky to adjust, they aren't fast (if you count all the times you have to start again and go over what you've done), they're messy, and unless you've had a lot of practice you'll end up with a terrible job (you should have stuck with the brush or aerosol). You can't get a good spray gun however much you pay and ones I've used professionally are a headache; without great skill you'll miss bits and get runs and bubbles (and insects stuck in the three square inches of the job that did come out right).

Anything sold with promises to rid your life of all work is a strong hint that you're getting some junk.

Then we have special nozzles for the garden hose (that we'd use once or twice a year, although a thumb over the end of the hose would probably work as well — then the nozzle has to be stored). Special spears and grips to get pickled onions out of the bottle without using our fingers (just how often do we have to get onions out of a bottle?); devices for cutting tomatoes to look like water lilies; complex grips for getting the lids off every size of jar known to man; garden seed spacers — and on and on and on. Gadgets may provide us with the glory of the moment, the convenience of the hour, but can end up being the plague of the day. Bigger, fancier, flashier is not always better.

Most of the miracle gadgets we end up hating because we were conned into buying them — but we refuse to get rid of them because we paid good money for them. We've been conned into believing that *convenience* is invariably desirable, even if it clutters our lives. This is junk hypnosis: if it's a gadget, shiny, attractive, easy to reach for, easy to pay for, we buy, accumulate and then shuffle it from cupboard to cupboard.

I'll bet every family has one or more exercise devices — exercise bikes, chest expanders, rowing machines, dumbbells. Exercise equipment for the most part — for old and young, flab and fat — is found in a drawer or on a shelf. The most exercise anyone ends up getting from it is moving it from one junk storage area to the next.

Then there is all the electrical junk. We presume that if anything is electric it must automatically be better and faster than manual. Don't you believe it! In the time we take to find and plug in the electric charcoal lighter (sandwich toaster, single hamburger maker, egg boiler) we could have done it easier and faster by hand. A lot of these things are a waste of good electric leads and not worth owning for their infrequent use. How many people actually use their electric card shufflers, electric sifters, electric carving knives, electric bottle warmers or electric toothbrushes?

Why were these things bought in the first place? Because they had an electric lead sticking out of them. I'll bet if you stuck an electric lead on a pair of chopsticks or knitting needles, there'd be a stampede for them!

Electronic things are superb to have and have made life much easier, but electronic isn't automatically better. High-tech is a degree of technology — not an assurance of efficient function. How comfortable you feel with things also has something to do with how useful they are to you. I still use an old manual typewriter. Beating hard on the keys releases my tensions and I can roll out reams of writing. Have you ever wondered what all those high-tech home computers are used for? Probably they're just an expensive way to play Pac-Man.

Remember, it's not just 'Is it faster or neater?' but 'How often will I use it?' that's the issue: you might want to think twice about that automatic stamp licker, hydraulic pillow fluffer-upper, self-starting orange peeler or electric ice cream scoop.

Accessories to the crime

I think the original intent of most accessories was to make a thing neater and easier to handle — is it working? Look at asparagus; it grew wild in the hedgerows and a few people picked it and ate it, no big deal. Then someone started inventing things to handle asparagus properly. . .

like special asparagus steamers, asparagus knives, asparagus ladles, asparagus racks, special string to tie up the stalks, special dishes to serve it in. The more gadgets to handle the wild weed of the hedgerow, the more prestige it gained — and the more expensive it got. Now the accessory entrepreneurs are trying this same approach on the good old egg: we have egg prickers, egg peelers, egg slicers, egg poachers, egg timers, egg turners, egg tongs, egg cozies, egg holders, egg slicers, egg separators, egg platters, and devilled egg rests. They're trying, with accessories, to do the same thing they did to asparagus: take it out of the hand of the common man by creating a whole special set of equipment for it.

Unreasonable attachments

As foods and gadgets sprout accessories, so do appliances. Most of us, for instance, have a love/hate relationship with our vacuum cleaners. Mostly we love the cleaner, we hate the attachments. The cleaner does ninety-eight per cent of the work; the miracle attachments (which we fell for after a salesman's fast talking) we seldom need or use — so they're shuffled around from cupboard to cupboard in their clever display box until the bottom falls out — then the attachments are thrown in a drawer, never to emerge again (except maybe as 'guess-whats' in a parlour game). We keep gadgets, even when the appliance they were attached to is defunct. That's almost as bad as keeping someone's new false teeth after he's died.

The attachment problem is compounded by the fact that machines today have so *many* attachments available. Besides a menacing array of shiny attachments for vacuums, there is a galaxy of glamorous sewing machine attachments — little bobbin adjusters, rufflers, seam stretchers, needle straighteners. My wife, who is an excellent dressmaker, has often commented that it's the accessories to a sewing machine that make everyone want one. Yet in producing the average dress or shirt or dressing gown, hardly one of these accessories is used. (By the time we find and fix one onto the machine, we could have done it faster and better with a needle and thimble.)

Knick-knacks

Many of us don't look at, use or even like our knick-knacks. Then why do we keep them? A few are true treasures; the rest of those hundreds of others, those tiny porcelain people, fanciful fowls and morose mammals, just sit there with insipid looks on their faces. The only time our interest is aroused much is when one of them gets knocked off and broken; then we wail and sob like a child. Our knick-knacks themselves become clutter collectors, demanding more and more shelves, stands, racks and cases to migrate to.

If your knick-knacks soothe you, give you inspiration, quicken your heartbeat at every touch, keep them. (But pitch the other 182 that don't.)

Behind closed doors

A cupboard is really the most logical place in the house to put the things we need to have handy. Cupboards are our most functional and valuable storage areas, but they are also the perfect convenient place to stash useless unneeded items out of sight. Cupboard junk is the most emotionally devastating because we see it many times a day..

How can you get your cupboards into good order? If the situation is really bad you could buy an enormous sack, stuff the contents of the cupboards into it and drag it off to the dump.

Seriously, though, I'd like to suggest here some junk-inhibiting practices you could adopt.

1. You start in a cupboard by de-cluttering it. That is the simple (and often heart-rending) process of getting rid of everything you don't use or need. We all know what is useless and what isn't.

2. Move the useful but used-once-or-twice-a-year (or every two to five years) stuff to a more remote (inactive) storage area. Remember, cupboards are your most accessible (active) storage area. Attics, lofts, or basement storage rooms are not, so transfer the worthwhile but not-frequently-used stuff (like camping gear, out-of-season clothes, scuba-diving masks, suitcases, etc.) to these areas.

3. Get stuff off the floor. Floor mess is about the most psychologically devastating of all messes. Most cupboards have a lot of unused space at the top — a few pounds worth of wood and a spare hour or two and you can install (or barter with a friend to install) a second or third shelf above the one over the clothes rail. This makes more room for worthwhile things you want to keep.

4. Hang everything you can on the wall. Remember, nothing — absolutely nothing — goes on the floor. If you are a person who rotates shoes or clothes, there are wall and other organizers you may find useful. Just use your head in choosing — and installing — storage

accessories or 'cupboard organizers'. Some do really help; others are just another kind of clutter.

5. Remember, *before* you stow things away is the best time to exercise control. (You'll never have the time to 'go back through it'.) Do you really *want* it? Do you *need* it? Does it have to go *there*? I realize most of us don't have enough cupboard space — but try, really try, not to pack too much into your cupboards. You'll defeat the purpose. No matter how cleverly you pack it all in and organize it — if a system won't stand up to quick, convenient use, it's ultimately doomed and will aggravate the mess.

Overcrowding makes it a lot harder both to get things out and to put them away. And you'll end up with a lot of re-ironing and re-pressing that shouldn't have been necessary.

Bathroom horror

The perfect miniature of the clutter-filled cupboard is the bathroom medicine cabinet. Let's just open the door and look inside. . .

Who convinced you to buy all this, anyway? It's unsafe, unsightly and uneconomical — and most of it is just dead weight; it doesn't really do anything for you. Some of the healthiest, happiest, handsomest people in the world survive without any of this. Starting and ending every day looking into this collection of clutter must surely affect your daily outlook, it might even *make* you feel ill. Old medicines and pills can be dangerous too, so have a ruthless throw out.

Coping with kiddie clutter

Most children, if given a chance, will de-clutter themselves. Little children, in particular, are great de-junkers; they play with or wear something until it falls apart or they lose interest (then they wisely break it, lose it or give it to a friend). But if we really work at it, we can teach our kids to be clutter collectors too. All it takes is intense examples from us grown-ups, constantly bombarding them with useless gifts and junkee ideas.

We owe our children better than this. If we let junk, litter and clutter become a constant condition in their lives, they'll get accustomed to it, feel comfortable with it — and later will duplicate the situation in their own cluttered lives and homes.

Some hints for controlling kiddie clutter

1. Much of kids' clutter is excess we've given them — get rid (or store and ring the changes) of those excess toys,

clothes, games, scooters; they won't miss them!

2. Give kids a place for their stuff. Growing people have their own belongings but most of the storage space in the house is taken by adult junk. If there's a place to put it, there's a sixty per cent better chance that it will get put away.

3. Lower cupboard and wardrobe rails so kids can hang things up easily.

4. Put casters on the toy box so the kids can pull it around to their disaster areas — it makes picking things up a lot easier and more likely.

Exterior junk

We all hate messy gardens — even someone whose garden looks like the city dump will, when viewing another sloppy rubbish strewn garden, purse his lips and say, 'What a disgrace, just look at all that rubbish, they must be real slobs.'

You feel the same way, don't you? But what is your garden like? Is it an eyesore? Junk starts right at the back door with rusted or broken washing machines, rotting bicycles, sagging gates, a slum birdhouse or two in condemned condition, a lean-to shed bulging with sun-cracked hoses, handleless tools, and rotting stakes and piles of cracked plant pots. And oh, yes — that pile of boards scrounged out of a junk pile, worn not from age, but from ten years of being moved around to more inconspicuous places. Let's not overlook the rusted swings, abandoned paddling pools, rusted grills from the barbecue set and the TV aerial that fell down during the worst storm of the '70s. Not to mention last year's Christmas tree saved for fire lighting and overgrown and untrimmed, dying and dead shrubbery.

Some back gardens are like an army obstacle course. The injuries possible from rubbish left lying in the garden don't bear thinking of. Worse still is the fact that so much of your potentially beautiful garden is so covered with junk that it can't be *used*. Just think — if you cleared it up you could do cartwheels on the lawn or have a picnic among the herbaceous borders! Messy gardens lower the tone of the area and affect property values. So set to and see what you can do to improve your immediate environment. Hire a skip and chuck the lot in — you'll be delighted with the space.

Garage clutter

The garage to most of us is a giant seasoning cellar for our debatable belongings. Yet it is a frequently used area. We leave from it to go to work or town and return through it, often with arms full of stuff, both coming and going. A garage is a very logical place to be kept in clean and useful condition.

It doesn't cost much to be de-cluttered. Here are a few ideas that will help.

1. A couple of planks and some breeze blocks can offer order, safety and convenience in the form of instant garage storage shelves for items that get a lot of use.

2. Store anything light by hanging it as high as reachably possible. This keeps it out of the stumbling-over path, yet readily accessible.

3. Find, buy or make a wall-hung cabinet to store paint, chemicals and other harmful substances.

4. If you wish to mount or hang frequently used tools the best way is to put up a 4x8-foot piece of quarter-inch pegboard on the wall. A variety of pegs and hooks are available.

5. Make sure you can see! Most garages are inadequately lighted, which makes them feel like a mine shaft instead of part of a home. The wiring is usually adequate; just install fluorescent tube lights in place of single bulbs. It will make the garage look better and will be safer and cheaper.

6. Paint the garage walls — ninety per cent of garages are unplastered, and thus look naked and shabby. Two coats of a good exterior emulsion can be applied for a few pounds and reward you for years.

7. Prepare and seal the floor, if it's concrete and has been down for at least thirty days. This will make it fast and easy to maintain and improve the looks and feel of the garage. Here's how: Remove all possible furniture, tools, etc., from the floor; sweep up all the surface dirt. Mop on a solution of strong alkaline cleaner, or better still, etching acid diluted in water. (Your DIY shop or supplier has these — make sure you follow the specific instructions on the label.) Let it soak in for a while; if the floor is old and marked you might want to scrub it with a floor scrubbing machine which can be hired. Wash the solution off, preferably using a floor squeegee, and rinse with a hose. Allow the floor to dry for at least five hours, then apply transparent concrete seal or an all-purpose seal, either of which can be obtained from a DIY shop or supplier. Apply the seal, according to the directions, with any applicator that will distribute it in a nice even coat, and let it dry. I'd advise a second coat to ensure good coverage.

Rural junkees

I don't like to single out any specific class or social order of junkee for dishonourable mention, but farmers deserve it (both men and women, so don't any of you try to sneak off). Everything written in this book about clutter can be applied 'double strength' to most farm people.

Farmers have one distinct advantage — or disadvantage, depending on how you view it — over town junkees: they have more room to spread it. They have silos, barns, sheds, cellars and granaries all available to store junk — and they do.

Farm men are almost twice as bad as farm women (who are twice as bad as normal town dwellers). Farmers keep *everything* because space is no problem — old tractors, machines and vehicles they just park farther out in the field each time. They keep them for parts, of course, and the ancient 1880 junk they keep to snare an unsuspecting townee who'll come along and pay good money for a rusty milk churn or a warped wagon wheel.

They have enough bolts buried somewhere to bolt down the cover on an MX missile, and as for tools, most have hundred of pounds worth. Yet they keep the wire and string from every bale of hay, and every bucket, can, barrel, sack and container that ever ambled onto the farm. Bits of wire, corrugated iron, old plastic sacks from fertilizer and feed stuffs, even though they can cause injury to livestock, are left lying in hedges and ditches. They never throw away a worn or broken part, because if the new one breaks, they can recycle the old one even twenty rusting years later.

Farm women, I love you — so I won't mention the fact that you are also the champion bottle collectors of the world, the garden junk accumulators of all time, the sewing scrap savers supreme, queens of the recipe collectors, and of course the cellar shelf fillers without equal.

Farmers, de-junk — and the local tip won't know what's hit it!

Chapter 7

Personal treasures

Don't think you're the only one who is in love with treasures you'll never use, treasures that are doing no good, but are unique, valuable and impress others with your good judgement for possessing them.

I have a handmade replica of the first Bell telephone, a pair of genuine maracas, a brass bugle and a collection of toilet novelties housed in a glass display case in my office.

At the age of twenty-one, on a trip abroad, I was fascinated by a little ship made out of seashells with thread rigging. I bought it because to me at the time it was a masterpiece to behold. I brought it home and moved it around, dusted it, cleaned it, repaired it. It sat on my shelf for twenty-seven years and had without doubt the finest physique to capture cobwebs of any object ever invented. The first five years I owned the thing I enjoyed it. The last twenty years were misery — it took something from me. Clutter of many kinds evolves in our life: without changing appearance it can quietly shift from a plus to a minus.

We are free agents when it comes to junking up our lives — we investigate, accumulate and then suddenly discover much of our lives is spent regulating the clutter we have accumulated. Clutter grows old quickly, and begins to irritate. Most people, when they reach the state of irritation, do the wrong things, go the wrong way; they accumulate more gadgets to help organize the clutter and that only leads to more clutter and more irritation.

Highbrow junk

Cost and *class* are not always partners. The word 'expensive' has whitewashed junk for far too long. We snigger aloofly at the cheap, ugly vase, while an elaborate engraved urn that does the very same thing (stands a flower up so we can smell it) gets the stamp of approval. The difference between porcelain and plaster of Paris here is insignificant; both are often obnoxious, seldom used, and not as attractive as a clean simple container

51

would be. Highbrow junk, we can call it. Those elegant gifts, or purchases — the lion claw candlesticks, silver cigarette lighters, chic little bowls, exotic lamps and copper or brass kitchen extras cost a lot more but are still in the same category as the cheap stuff.

Many of these inexpressibly elegant things don't actually *do* anything — they are pure decoration, exquisite objects that just *sit* in a house — which is fine if you really enjoy them, take real *pleasure* in looking at them and rearranging their display. But junk is junk if you don't take much notice of it, and it has no real useful purpose.

Sold as brass

'Brass' and 'copper' are important words in the highbrow junk vocabulary. A woman I overheard commented that every time her husband came back from a foreign country, he brought her something — it didn't really matter what, as long as it was *brass*. She complained, said that she could start a metal recycling foundry in her living room, but he continued bringing things home because they were not only a bargain, they were *brass!*

Brass and copper *are* durable, but not necessarily better for every purpose and they are high-maintenance materials. They cost a small fortune to buy and a bigger fortune in time to keep looking good. I once helped clean King Charles II's 350-year-old brass candleholders in Winchester Cathedral. Those massive, elegant things are worn thin and frail from being polished once a week for all those years. Even the solder is wearing out from cleaning. How many lifetimes have been polished away in that time? Do any personal treasures take precedence over human life — especially yours?

Elaborate, overdone furniture is a must on the highbrow clutter collector's list. These things are designed, built and sold to be looked at. I can enjoy eating at a nice big handsome table — but I have a hard time understanding how and why people will queue up and pay to look at a table. 'It's a Chippendale,' someone gasps. So what?

Another fixture of highbrow junk is the twinkling crystal chandelier. As a professional cleaner, I hate them. Light is light, and rarely can a person tell the difference between polished plastic and crystal yet crystal, like china, seems to be bought mainly to lend an elegance to the household that the dwellers seem to lack.

You could easily argue that highbrow junk is *more* immoral than lowbrow junk because it's more expensive both to buy and to care for. We could have spent that money to feed a starving child or help a struggling student, to fund a cause, friend, family — something alive! We can satisfy our junking impulse in a big spree down the high street and not feel too bad — we may have a pile of awful things but we're only down £25 or less. Highbrow junk costs hundreds or thousands of pounds and we can *still* have a pile of awful stuff.

China and silverware displays

Some clutter seems to be used to resolve a family identity hang-up. Classic examples are china and silverware. To accumulate that one special set of china and silver (right down to the embossed silver ladle) is a lifetime dream of many. When they finally get it all, there's no way they'll risk breaking, scratching or losing any of it. So a horror of a china cabinet is acquired and therein — behind glass — is the treasure. The silver is velvet-draped in an oak casket, double-locked in the bottom drawer of the same cabinet.

Who in their right mind would really take all this space, time, trouble and insurance money to display a set of *tableware?* Think about it — a display of eating tools — so people can gaze and say, 'Oh, your saucer is so captivating. Is it Crown Derby or Royal Doulton?' If we're going to display some household implement, why not something with more character — like the tin opener, potato masher, even the garden spray nozzle? Most 'good' china is used once or twice a year; silverware less. It takes tons of energy to keep it clean and sparkling. After you die someone will probably end up feeding their old hound dog out of it anyway. Those place settings would pay for a holiday or an education that would nourish you much more than any food eaten off them ever will!

Hobbies and collections

Some of the most worthwhile and inspiring achievements in the world come from people who gathered, preserved, restored and displayed things and appreciated their greatness. But the value of this whole undertaking is in *sharing* it — displayed (or otherwise used) hobbies and collections stimulate our fellow humans and inspire them to accomplishment.

As long as a collection produces those effects, it's probably a plus, but think of how many 'collections' end up out of bounds and out of sight. The model train that took a space on the floor. . . then the room. . . then the adjoining room. . . The dog and the children get smacked for fiddling or playing with it. Our glass or jewellery collection often gets too valuable to be used or left where it can be seen and we wouldn't think of selling it — so what value is it? A time, space and energy robber!

It can't be denied that some of us get a (perhaps not admirable) thrill out of simply acquiring, hoarding, counting, running our fingers over, polishing — all by our own personal selves — our *collections*. If it really adds to our life, then it

is of unquestionable value; this again is why 'junk or not' is a judgement only you can make.

Antiques

We all cherish the history, character and spirit that antiques convey. They look great on display in museums or mounted in galleries or put to use in homes, but when our whole house becomes a 'don't touch' antique asylum, we may want to reassess our 'valuable' merchandise. Is it just for show or status or is it an 'I got it first' ego object? If so, it will clutter up your life. Donate it to a museum and get them to engrave your name on a plate and fasten it to the case. You'll get full credit, thousands will see it and it will last many of your lifetimes (that's more than you were accomplishing with it around the house).

One of the biggest problems with antiques is that we all have a friend or have read an article that tells us we have a fortune under those cobwebs. When I worked with teams of horses as a youth, old worn-out horse collars were of no value, and we threw them away. So when I saw a collar with a mirror mounted in it, price-tagged at £150 — I was sick; I'd thrown away at least £1500 worth of horse collars! From then on I resolved to save all old farm stuff. Six sheds full later with still no one beating a path to my door, I realized I was deceiving myself.

Why are people fascinated by and why do they long for the old, the quaint, the antique? They want to retreat to, be reminded of, be projected back to a simpler day of greater freedom and integrity — they secretly want to be *de-junked!*

Junk doesn't generate self-esteem

It has been observed that people (rich and poor) who keep themselves and their homes overloaded with things often have extremely low self-esteem. Many are professional people, astute holders of public offices etc., but they don't seem to measure up to what they're trying to be. They have tons of 'in' or 'proper' things but seldom ever *use* them — the stuff is just displayed like banners or flags, a kind of testament of intention. These people have jogging suits but they don't jog, exercise bikes that are rusting away, how-to-discipline-children books but unruly kids, and tons of sports or fishing or camping gear but they never play, sport or fish or camp. They buy cookery books to assuage their guilt for never cooking. By owning and surrounding themselves with the trappings, they somehow satisfy the need to be what people expect them to be.

Often the best-equipped, best-prepared person is the one who does the least.

A friend of mine once bought a 790-piece tool set; he never turned a bolt, but it made him feel he was *equipped* to do anything that might come up.

Junk doesn't generate self-esteem or fulfil our ambitions — only *we* can do that. 'Owning' is like theory, totally worthless if not put to use. Sitting there in idle beauty, clutter can in fact *undermine* our self-esteem — all those 'I ought, but I don'ts' will get you every time they're brought to sight or mind.

How do you judge value?

Judgements on the worth or worthlessness of things are, in the end, your business, not mine as the writer of this book. I'll be satisfied if I manage to make you stop and think about, weigh up the worth of some of the 'valuables' you hoard, guard, polish and display.

Don't be like the father who had four antique guns — not one-of-a-kind collector's items, but respectable pieces worth about £5,000 each. When his daughter reached college age, the family was short of money and could see no way to pay £5,000 per year to see their vibrant and musically talented daughter fulfil her education and her dream. She never did, and the father kept those old guns in a rack until he died. Then the kids divided them up, sold them, bought cars and couches, and threw parties. His daughter could have been a living inspiration for all his posterity; his guns ended up valueless.

Capital clutter

Money was once a medium of exchange; somehow it has come to be a measure of personal value. Of course money is needed for sustenance and some convenience, but the time and energy we spend on handling it and keeping it can easily be the most catastrophic clutter in our lives.

Once I used to watch the financial 'geniuses', read the financial books and papers, and pay close attention to the classy ads and articles. I spread my money around, dealt with several banks, and had a spot of money in this investment and a spot in that investment and some in different savings accounts.

The balancing and paperwork to keep up these financial appearances ('image') wasn't worth it. All those accounts and investments cluttered up my life; it was a total waste of time and space. I finally found one banker I liked and got rid of my numerous accounts.

Like magic my postage and accounting costs and the time spent fiddling round with numerous little financial matters shrank.

People who make commission out of you are experts — when they know you can't afford something, financially or emotionally, they work out a method of payment so you can get it. Fifteen percent return on something that strains a relationship, a marriage or your health is a poor investment.

The polite man's burden: gifts

Christmas, Easter, birthdays, Valentine's Day, goodbyes, hellos always inspire a gift, of cash or sentimental value. It's the thought that counts, of course, but once the thought is registered, we still have the item hanging around. We all worry that the giver might see the gift in the bin if we throw it out, or that they'll be hurt if we don't display or use it. Well, they probably will be, but getting rid of the stuff would help eliminate daily irritation in your life.

What is the value of a gift?

A gift, regardless of its value, if given sincerely has a certain sacredness. It is a concise message of love and appreciation, a nod of acknowledgement for something felt. But we should always remember not to confuse the *meaning* of a gift with the gift itself. The actual gift is only a vessel to express; once it does that, generally it has fulfilled its function. Its message will live with us, be part of us — forever, possibly — but should we drag around the vessel after it has served its purpose? That's like leaving the scaffolding up after a building is finished — take it down!

Once on return from a trip I bought my wife a dozen red roses. They showed how I cared about her. For several days they were a joy and when they withered they were thrown out with no regrets.

Returning from another trip I spent a similar sum of money on a huge toy dog. Initially it gave the same amount of pleasure but after a year or two, tattered and sagging, it was a huge encumbrance. What a relief it was when we gave it to a little boy who adored it.

Think of the things you have received or given that cost even less than meals, roses, perfumes, etc., that are long gone, but that you got your money's worth and more out of even though you have nothing physical left to show for it. Many of the things that bring fun or enjoyment to our lives, promote good will, give us a good thrill, or carry a caring message are not *objects*. So why keep every trinket? You don't have to keep them to prove anything. The memories and feelings aren't in the gifts, but in *you*, and a tangible gift can actually become a junk millstone around your neck.

Dare to be really different

We all like to be unique in our personality and possessions, and this 'individualism' contributes greatly to clutter accumulation. We'll search unrelentingly for something 'different' — for us, or for a gift. Giving the unusual is the highest standard of gift giving. The harder to find, the rarer, the odder, the greater the mystique, the greater our points, score and (regardless of its worth) the more greatly it is valued. An object's actual use or contribution is no consideration here — only the fact that 'no one else has one'. This is why those catalogues crammed with monogrammed toilet paper, electric bookmarkers, talking lamps and walking false teeth are so compelling.

What happens to such things after the giddy moment of presentation is generally ignored. The 'different' thing is among the most eligible to become junk. To really be different, let's not waste each other's time and money on them. I won't dump any on you if you won't on me, because we'll both have trouble discarding them.

Can charity be uncharitable?

We've all fallen once or twice for the tempestuous acquisition of a gift for no one in particular. We spot something we want, we don't really *need* it, we can't really afford it, it doesn't suit us one hundred per cent — but it's lovely: we want it. Our conscience sides with dejunking and tells us no! — but it's so *nice* (it could be a simple clay pot or a slab of salmon). We finally resort to Scripture, which tells us charity is the most honourable of human acts, so we get it 'to give to someone.' Now that we have bought it without guilt, one of three things will happen:

1. We will never give it to anyone.

2. If we *do* give it to someone we hold dear, we'll have to give them another gift on top of it (because we know *they* don't really want it).

3. We'll end up giving it to someone we had no intention of giving anything to. We really aren't being kind — we're making *ourselves* feel better.

Listen to your conscience — IT KNOWS!

When giving gifts, don't saddle the recipient with something useless. Ralph Waldo Emerson gave some good guidelines for a gift:

The only gift is a portion of thyself. Thou must bleed for me. Therefore the poet brings his poem; the shepherd, his lamb; the farmer, corn; the miner, a gem; the sailor, coral and shells; the painter, his picture; the girl, a handkerchief of her own sewing. This is right and pleasing, for it restores society in so far to its primary basis, when a man's biography is conveyed in his gift, and every man's wealth is an index of his merit. But it is a cold, lifeless business when you go to the shops to buy me something which does not represent your life and talent, but a goldsmith's.

How to dispose of junk gifts

Give it to someone else down the line in the family who might actually need it. 'Passed for posterity' is usually accepted *within* a family.

You can take a colour picture of the gift — then take the gift to the Oxfam shop. The picture is evidence that you must have appreciated it — after all, who would photograph junk?

You can leave it in your car, on the back seat (gift-wrapped if necessary), and park your car, unlocked, in a rough part of town. If it doesn't disappear quickly, leave the window open a little. When you tell the giver the gift was literally stolen from your car, they will be flattered that (1) you were carrying it around, and (2) someone wanted it enough to steal it. That's double value — triple if you count your relief.

You can put your name on a gift and donate it to a museum — that really turns the giver on: they'll love you as much as you love getting rid of the thing. You could donate it to an auction (just make sure it's in another town).

If you let it be known that you don't like expensive gifts, or that it is against company or personal policy to accept gifts, it's amazing how quickly gifts stop.

As a last resort, go and join a religious order, make a pilgrimage, take on a mission! Anything you rid yourself of in the name of the Lord will never be questioned.

Or you can write a book on clutter — it's amazing how fast people stop giving you trinkets. My last birthday found me in the middle of editing this book; at supper my two daughters and wife confessed they had no present for me; they'd looked for four hours and found nothing I hadn't attacked in this volume. The fact that they had spent four hours flattered me — what a gift — I loved it! We all benefited! My mother sent me a cassette on which she'd taped my favourite violin music, another daughter phoned from Ottawa, my son-in-law baked some trout he'd caught, my granddaughter gave me a card she'd crayoned, and my oldest daughter bottled me fourteen jars of fresh raspberries. I've treasured that birthday as my best ever!

Homemade... makes it hard

Homemade, with their own hands, from the heart — even the most heartless de-junker flinches when trying to dispose of that solid chipboard bedstead or that pink and purple Mother's Day apron the kids made during the holidays or at school. Show me a daddy, mummy, grandpa or grandma who can easily part with even the most obnoxiously made handicraft. Besides being hard to lift, those precious handmade shoe polish boxes, plaster hand casts, coffee tables and jewellery boxes are as durable as granite and will survive six generations. Once made, you're stuck: since you usually don't want to be seen with them, they don't have a chance to wear out or get broken. Deep in my heart I have a solid respect for what schools and clubs produce from a bunch of kids. They embalm a pile of lollipop sticks with white glue and they become indestructible. Earthquake, flood or fire — they will

survive it all. And of course, no one in their right mind would steal them.

What's the solution? I'm stumped, and I have a two-pound tooled leather keychain, a three-inch-thick wooden soap holder, a painted rock and a pine-cone panther mounted on a slab of three by two wood staring me in the face at the moment. If there are unusually tender feelings involved, it's probably worth making the sacrifice and using it — it's no worse than telling someone how great his or her cooking is when it is practically inedible.

What about trophies and awards?

Helping others, winning, succeeding, participating, playing, working, attending or entering just about anything is likely to earn you a trophy or award. These come in the form of certificates, badges, plates, plaques, figurines, bookends and desk sets.

Trophies and awards, like gifts, are basically a 'thank you', a tangible affirmation of success or excellence. It's a thrill to get one, no doubt about it. But if you are really good and get better, you'll get more and more and more — and you'll end up needing an entire room to hold and display them all.

At my numerous 'Is there life after housework' seminars I receive all kinds of gifts, from groups and individuals, ranging from miniature flowers to bronzed toilet brushes. I appreciate these things, but what do you do with so many things? I'm a little chary of people who have to cover their walls with certificates and awards. If you've got it or had it, it should show in your personality and the way you present yourself. Glory is nebulous but the strength of character and body you developed on your way to earning the award is yours. It's not junk, but a life-giving resource.

Don't take old trophies and awards too seriously. Most of them look as though they were carved or cast out of one of the same three moulds anyway, and they tarnish, tear, tip over and provide a landing strip for flies; you end up spending most of the athletic or creative skill you earned them with now manipulating them.

Cull out the dead ones and keep the living; and review the situation from time to time.

Consider *giving* them away — let your kids, grandchildren and your neighbours' children get pleasure from them as toys or rewards for chores or heroics. Children are smart enough to wear it out or lose it. This is also a good place to make use of the photograph technique: take a good sharp photo of it, and part with it.

And if you're *giving* an award, try to remember that trophies are basically useless. An axe can chop and be useful; a trophy with a golden axe on top is good for nothing. Give a living award — films, tapes, equipment, clothing, money, trips — not a shrine that must be tended.

58

What to keep of the keepsakes

There comes a time when memories and the tokens of memories have to be separated. On a thing as personal as a keepsake it can only be your decision what to throw out. I offer just one guideline before you start:

Don't love what can't love you back.

We all want to cherish a good memory or experience forever, but preoccupation with physical reminders can lead us to live in the past. One of the toughest and most necessary things in the world for growth and happiness is to release our hold on things, places, and people we've outgrown. Too many people never grow and gain expanding new experiences because they can't see the wisdom of releasing old ones. Junk squeezes out new life.

Aftermath junk

Be sure you distinguish keepsakes from aftermath junk — which has got to be about the sickest junk of all. This consists of keeping something to remind you of a terrible experience, like the knife that cut the tendon in your hand, that old plaster cast, your kidney stones, your ex-boyfriend's insulting letter and even his frayed jacket.

With all the new life and love out there, constantly resurrecting old suffering memories is really straining for something to do in our spare time. When you stop dragging the skeletons of the past, the once-was or once-did with you, you'll have more freedom to love and be loved. Free yourself from clutter at the critical moment when what you are giving to it outweighs what you are gaining *from* it. De-junking is the easiest and most rewarding way to change a dull life to a positive life.

When it comes to keepsakes, ask only one question: *For whom are you keeping it?* Who is the documentation for — you? *You* don't need proof — you *experienced* it. Meaning isn't kept in things, but in memory.

There is no possession finer than a good memory of something. You can use it over and over again, it can make your pulse quicken, your heart sigh, bring tears of joy to your eyes or a laugh to your day — and a good memory of something costs nothing to keep.

Can posterity... be preposterous?

Preserve for posterity, but don't become a posterity pervert. Too often our efforts to record an event for posterity end up reducing its significance.

Take weddings, for example — too often, the whole ceremony has to be scheduled and conducted around the formalities of pictures, bridesmaids, souvenir-saving and speeches. The photographers seldom stand back and take a real action photo of the occasion; they halt the ceremony and move people around according to height, relationship, seniority and what-have-you. Everyone is so bent on preserving, they never savour the actual rapture of the moment — they have to look at the pictures to actually experience the event.

Experiences are meant to be just that — an actual live experience. They shouldn't be prerecorded to be 'aired' later in life. I've watched people at beauty spots so bent on collecting 'records' to enjoy later, they missed the beauty of the landscape. They were so buried in junk food, so busy taking pictures, buying souvenirs, T-shirts and maps to the next site that they never took a minute to stand and soak up the actual experience of that spectacular place.

Your last gift: don't junk from the grave

Everyone over fifty spends too much time and emotion worrying about what they'll leave to their family; everyone under fifty spends too much time and emotion worrying about what they're going to inherit. It's downright stupid. Leaving possessions to a family is often more an act of revenge than love. It's pathetic how families are broken apart, divided into a mass of quarrelling maniacs squabbling and sueing over dead people's junk. Oddly enough, it's usually not the normal inheritances of land or money that everyone gets most uptight about — it's the ordinary possessions, the stuff only valuable to the person who previously owned and treasured it.

Inheriting the hoard

Think for a minute — what will happen to all of *your* belongings, those stored sentimental personal items, when you pass away? Someone, someday will have to come and unappreciatively wade through it. To you, most of it is treasure; to them, it's trash. They'll feel guilty disposing of it because it's *yours*.

Don't burden someone else with your junk. Spend it, give it away, sell it — don't leave for heaven without it. Cash in your clutter before *you* cash in — start at the age of forty-five just to be safe.

How would you like your obituary to read like this:

She is survived by: twenty four Beatles posters; thirty bags of fabric scraps for patch work; a bullworker; a purple flower arrangement; twenty pairs of babyshoes; seven hundred copies of *Good Housekeeping;* an assortment of old badges; fifty-six lidless cottage cheese cartons; fourteen half-finished needlepoint projects; eleven matted teddy bears; two boxes of unfiled recipes; a dried-up china-painting kit; seventy-three empty cigar boxes; a jug of pennies; a ping pong bat; a box of Christmas cracker mottoes; and every birthday card she was ever given.

Taming the paper tiger

We are inundated daily with displays of reading matter — signs, menus, magazines, maps, papers, programmes, brochures, labels, newsletters, books. We don't have to ask for it or buy it — it comes spontaneously, generously, regularly, much of it free. Seventy-five per cent of it is or will quickly become clutter, and will smother the life out of us if we don't exercise some kind of control over it.

Everyone keeps old magazines and newspapers but what about all those less obvious bits of paper? Have you ever noticed how most people keep expired life-insurance policies? Just in case reincarnation might occur in reverse. We paid so much for it. It looks so 'legal'. We'd better keep it.

The other faithful piece of paper junk never thrown out is the old raffle ticket; the fact that we keep it, though the draw was in 1965, indicates that human hope truly never dies (as long as we keep junk around to remind us of it).

How much unopened junk post, how many outdated catalogues and newsletters, obsolete timetables, old lists, worn out slogan stickers, wrinkled posters and old greetings cards and calendars, half-filled-out questionnaires, old competition entry forms and magazine subscription offers, outdated reports, box tops, expired coupons and unidentifiable envelopes of stuff do you have stashed somewhere? (Probably under all your old fishing and driver's licences, or those eighteen never-used diaries.) What about ancient books of addresses and names of associates — met once, a long time ago? Will you ever use them, or will they pile up and crowd out new friends and opportunities? All those handwritten notes awaiting translation might be memoir-excusables — but not the mounds of catalogues bulging out of every nook. (I know a well-educated woman who has over six hundred assorted catalogues.)

The 'paper weight' in our lives from keeping all this undiscarded print is a psychological ton. We can't shake the conviction that we are morally obliged to read, or at least scan it before the rubbish truck bears it away forever. But remember, seventy-five per cent of it is obsolete hours after it's printed, and after ten years, I think the other twenty-five per cent has given up the ghost. Dump it! Don't give the old 'I'm waiting for the Boy Scout paper collection' alibi — attack that paper. If you collect over a thousand pounds in weight, call me — I've got to see it!

Junk post — or even 'good post' that ends up junk — is one of the most universal junk problems. It is stuffed, hidden, spread, stacked, piled, stored, filed, boxed and even carried around in such abundance in most homes and offices that it's actually physical labour to handle, as well as an emotional drain to keep track of Desk tops can't be found, bulging boxes are piled in cupboards, drawers are so bunged up with junk post they can't be opened. Most of this out of date post is worthless and is silently destroying some of your finest nerve fibre,

and taking up some of your most valuable house space.

The 'ostrich approach' to the post stream can and does hurt employment, relationships and the pocket. It can represent you as a person unable to handle personal responsibilities. Dealing with post and magazines is one of the most shamefully deferred jobs of all. Instead of feeling bad about it, set to and tackle it.

You can handle junk post in minutes

Let me help you sort. You don't have to do it like I do — you can adjust the process to suit yourself — but here are some guidelines to expedite the task.

Never throw anything away before you look at it. It is sound economic sense to advertise, sell and offer, and you should give *some* consideration — however brief — to what is sent or said to you. I once ripped up and threw away an envelope that appeared to be an insurance advertisement, only to find out later that it was a cheque for £1,000 I'd been waiting for.

Magazines are fun to read and the stories and ads keep you aware of what's new, but remember a couple of things.

1) In most magazines, nothing is printed that is too profound or controversial or they would lose advertisers; most magazine material, while perhaps enjoyable, is not fantastically edifying to the mind.

2) Up to seventy per cent of a magazine is advertisements and they are updated every month, so you don't need to keep them. You can go through a trade journal or newsletter in minutes, scanning the headlines. If there happens to be an article

you want to read or save, tear it out and read or file it, and throw the rest away — it's pure rubbish. Yet people store tons of magazines. What value is a ninety-pound box of 1968-72 *Better Biscuits and Garters?* Seventy per cent is out-of-date ads; most of the rest is obsolete or out-of-style ideas.

When it comes to magazines, a little hard thinking while you're poised over the subscription form can save a lot of guilt and accumulation later. Are you *really* going to read it? Or do you just want it to be seen in your house or office?

And because you paid for it doesn't mean you have to read it. If you miss something, there's a good chance you'll be able to read it a year later in the doctor's waiting room, because receptionists seem to keep magazines even longer than you do.

Bills — the most dreaded. In almost every home I cleaned in twenty-five years as a professional, there was a little den or pile of unpaid (and unopened) bills. Always open every bill immediately — never throw away or file one because you haven't the money to pay it. Many of us have suffered for this. I had one for six months; I didn't open it because I didn't want to know how much it was for, and when I did it was worse than I thought. In fact, it was a rip-off on some building work I'd had done. I yelled my head off about the £250 they had overcharged, but to no avail because six months had gone by — wheat had grown over the proof. I 'hid' another bill from myself for months when money was desperately tight; I worried, sweated, and finally opened it — to find it was a credit for £200, asking how I'd like it, cash or a cheque. If you can't take care of all your bills, at least be aware of to whom, how much and when they have to be paid. Instant adjustment to the shock is

less damaging than long-unknowing suspenseful agony. Don't keep bill inserts; they're bulky and usually irrelevant — all you need is the statement or invoices, and if you insist, the envelope.

Competitions Just rub off the plastic cover, peel to reveal the hidden code, or simply match the numbers. And what do we win. . . a drawer full of false hope. . . scrap paper. We keep the labels, cards and coupons in case we stand to win the £50,000 jackpot. We don't and the postman brings us more and more and ever more junk post, as our name is computer-plucked from mailing lists for future junk bombardment. When a real opportunity for fame and fortune comes through our door, we miss it because we can't see over the pile of entries on the kitchen table.

Sorry I'm so hard on this, but I think postal competitions are almost immoral. Giving nothing and getting lots just doesn't work and never will. Hoping for something for nothing, which most competitions encourage, will junk up your life. We waste a lot of valuable time and emotion dreaming and hoping — and even if we were the .000001 per cent that win, our troubles would just be starting. Many of the prizes are things we don't want or need, and winning a holiday (or a lifetime) with nothing to do would ruin most of us.

Complete the following sentence in twenty-five words or less:

Junk post piles up in my house because.......
....
....

Deals and offers

When people have to solicit us for a deal, it is definitely not as good a deal as we could go after on our own. There are plenty of deals in the post, good and bad ones among them. The best investment opportunities are seldom announced in circulars. Most of them you can throw away especially if they start: 'You have been selected. . . '

There seems to be magic in the word 'investment', especially when we read rags-to-riches stories, how-I-gained-power tales, and 'how by investing five minutes a week I made a million pounds, gained a master touch on the piano, this bustline or that bicep'.

In this frame of mind we're set up for a plunge into the pool of gimmicks, not investments. Our world has fast become one big sphere of promise. Almost every person, company, group, organization or government is constantly, twenty-four hours a day, trying to get us to invest in something. In the course of an average week in our life we'll be exposed to a hundred opportunities to improve life, gain a friend, see the world, master our emotions or make money. All we have to do is say 'Yes', then pay up, and wait for our ship to come in. . . A great opportunity? No! On many of these investments there isn't even a ship sailing — you can be swindled. It happens fast; it happens often.

Make-money-at-home junk post is awesome. There are hundreds of such schemes. When someone promises to make you a Rolls Royce-driving millionaire with no work, no investment, no selling, no risk, for a £10 formula, you are being insulted, not approached. If small fortunes were being made quietly at home raising earthworms, knitting nosewarmers or stuffing envelopes, it wouldn't be a secret long. Thousands of people reply in the hope of financial solutions and send in some of the little

money they do have, as the ad asks them to. Be careful — a dotted line can make a junk transfer in seconds.

Many of those direct-sales, 'pyramid' fortune-building outfits promising something for nothing are among the biggest junk concepts in the world. Few ever make it. But homes and offices are littered with glorious brochures showing smiling families posed in front of their big shiny car and landscaped garden, proof that by using others you, too, can build a fortune.

Readers' clubs

I read the coaxing, colourful ads for years and finally a book popped up that I wanted. It was free just for joining. I signed the coupon and the gate swung open and those paper goodies didn't stop. I'd read the catalogue and find nothing I wanted so they'd send me *their* choice (*The History of Masking Tape*). I'd get so irritated that on the next offer, before they could just send me A *Rudder Study of the Great Sailboats*, I'd order it. I tried to get rid of my book club purchases as Christmas gifts, but others were doing the same and I ended up with gift copies of the same books I'd gleefully given away.

I stuck with the club for five years — do you realize how many months there are in five years? The books and extras were pretty, but seldom really edifying (or read). It was hard to get out because I felt guilty about getting that free book when I joined, but finally, after being thoroughly deluged, I withdrew.

Feeling relieved, de-junked, unburdened from that monthly pressure, I still hadn't learned my lesson. A business book library offer came (what a clever way to disguise the *real* name — book club) and I fell for it. These were different, however — they cost £25 instead of £7.95

each and my corporate name was peddled to every mailing list and merchant in the US I really opened the flood gate this time — I had catalogues arriving hourly selling surplus Army jeeps, sexual aids, pewter paraphernalia, electronic dominoes, stretch covers, insurance and double glazing. I never did read any of the big complicated business books, but the catalogues usually each had one item I might buy one day, so I kept them. In two years I could have opened my own paper recycling plant.

Catalogues Allowing sleek, slick catalogues, large and small, steadily to enter your dwelling is like touring the bakery when you're starting a diet.

Our fascination with the glossy anthologies of clutter called catalogues knows no bounds. The new ones pile up and take time we don't have to go through and discover new things we wouldn't have needed or wanted if we hadn't seen them there in all their full-colour and backdropped glory. The old ones pile up because we never get round to wading back through them to weed out.

Catalogues not only add to our *paper* clutter, they have (in those innocent-looking little order forms) the incredible potential to multiply every other kind of clutter on our premises astronomically.

Letters Open immediately, and if the address and date are on the letter, throw the envelope away. Read the letter, and if it doesn't call for a reply, throw it away or file it or save the address or make out a cheque or whatever and get rid of it. If it needs an answer, carry it with you until you answer it. That will be the best disciplined and most efficient way to make sure you do.

One of the most valuable skills of time management is learning to use time

fragments — the ten minutes queueing up, the twenty minutes waiting for a meal, the thirty minutes travelling somewhere, etc. Letter-answering is an excellent way to do this.

Old letters aren't always clutter, neither are special cards and notes and postcards — they are human history. The letters that bring tears to our eyes and a flood of memory and love may be old and yellow, but never junk. Meaningful writings are easy to store and the amount of feeling they hold is well worth the space. If necessary, trim them down to get rid of the bulk.

I cut out the most meaningful parts of my favourite letters, laminate them and insert them in books as markers. When I open the book — monthly, yearly or every five years — there the letter is, in perfect condition, to remind me.

Calendars You only need a couple of calendars in a house, yet after Christmas we have one for each month. Because of the friends who gave them, or the fact that they came in the post or were given to us *free*, we feel obliged to keep all calendars and they end up being clutter. Our digital watches, TV and newspapers remind us almost hourly what day and year it is; don't take or keep calendars if you don't need them — they cost the distributor a lot and you'll never be able to throw them away because of all those pretty pictures.

Wall planners

The 'big calendar' idea used by home efficiency experts is a wonderful way to eliminate junk post, unnecessary phone calls and clutter.

A big calendar is one with the days marked off in squares big enough to write notes inside. Purchase the one with the largest squares you can find. Hang it on the wall next to your telephone and notice board (if your notice board isn't next to the telephone, move it!), near the heaviest flow of communication. Put a pen or pencil on a string or in a slot beside your calendar. From now on, as soon as invitations and anouncements arrive in the post or are brought home, instead of hanging onto them (but never being able to find them when you need the information), simply transfer the data (address, time, etc.) onto the appropriate square of your big calendar, then throw the card or circular out before it can clutter your house — and clutter your mind trying to keep track of it!

Place a wastepaper basket on the floor beneath your big calendar and watch the basket fill up with that flurry of junk you formerly had been saving, shuffling, hunting for and worrying about. Things like wedding and party invitations, notifications of events, timetables, appointment cards and reminders, loose addresses of places you're going to, meetings, instructions, letters containing specific information, etc., etc. — often we have our desk drawers stuffed full of this junk. We cram these things in our wallets or handbags or put them on the refrigerator to 'remind' us of things we need to do. It's so messy and confusing — and so unnecessary — to keep it all around.

A great feeling of power comes from feeling in control of your life's events, from knowing what's coming up and where you've been. Big calendars can help you achieve that control at a quick glance.

If your mechanic tells you the brakes should be checked again in six months, flip ahead on your calendar and write in the check-up date. If your insurance falls due twice a year, don't always be caught unawares. Pencil in reminders to yourself so you can budget ahead and have the money available.

Write in important birthdays and dates a year ahead, then mark reminders to yourself a week before so you can get the greetings card off in time.

Hang onto your big calendars and file them. They're a concise record of family history. They tell you everything you and your family did all year and exactly when you did it.

File it doesn't mean pile it

Files are one of the greatest repositories of 'invisible' clutter going — just because it's in alphabetical order and tucked away in a drawer doesn't mean it isn't junk.

My values and needs change, as yours do, as the years pass and the tenor of my life changes, but seldom do I go back into my files and throw out the clutter and stuff that no longer applies because 'it would take forever'. And besides, you say, you can throw it out when you happen to come across it when you're looking for something else.

Well, it won't happen, and your files will grow into a Whitehall paper storage bank that makes retrieving anything (*if* you can find it) slow and costly. Yet it takes only minutes, while you're watching TV or when you can't get to sleep one evening or your match is rained off — to sit down and riffle through some of your files. This is fun, educational and reminds you how clever you are for saving all this stuff. If you throw clutter away periodically, your files will stay healthy and when you need something you won't have to mount an expedition or perform an excavation to get it. Office or home, *you* have to do it: if someone else cleans out your files, that is exactly what they might do — clean them out, and there goes the picture of you forty eons or so ago, the masterful letter that proved you weren't speeding, your grandfather's letter from Winston Churchill.

Without a functional filing system, finding and using can be a maddening and disappointing quest. But there is such a thing as over-organizing — when you have to use a separate set of files to find where something was filed or otherwise put away.

File to fit your personality and needs — don't try to follow the Dewey system invented for the American University Library. Surprisingly few folders or notebooks can organize almost anything you need and do it well. Don't stuff things in a drawer — that simple file or folder, with a title or subject written across the top, will only take a minute to make and will cost under a pound. When you need it, you'll be able to find it.

Basements, bits and bobs

Losing track of something we liked and saved is almost as sad as losing a cherished memory of a loved one: snatching gems of thought out of the torrent of life is one of our great pleasures. Develop your own system to make sure you save and *use* them. Your method will have to suit *you*.

My system isn't sophisticated, but it works, and this is all I do: I save everything that impresses me (five to fifty snippets a day). I carry a leather notebook with a pouch and a pad — everything I collect or jot down goes in one of these.

I write out my notes on the spot in my notebook on a sheet titled 'Write & Record'. I write each separate thought out in complete sentences under a key word or subject heading. I don't go into full detail or describe it completely, just enough so that if I *do* want to go back to expand on it I'll know clearly what I meant. Writing down the notes only takes a minute, if done right at the moment the thought strikes.

When I get home I drop all my Write & Record notes (snipped into their separate subjects into a box labelled 'Write & Record', and drop all the printed materials, programmes, photos, documents, forms, booklets, etc., I've picked up into the 'Important Paper' basket on my desk. This way I have all my notes and gleanings in one of two places — not in pockets, bags, boxes, books, all over the place.

I don't use prime time — such as morning hours — to file the material in these two boxes; this can be done in time fragments, when you're not feeling too well, while watching TV or looking after the kids, while waiting for someone, before and just after meals, on sleepless nights, etc.

My files are arranged so that I have a drawer for each of my important interests and one alphabetical 'general' file drawer. My immediate-interest projects/current enthusiasms I keep in ring binders — such topics, for me, for example, as The Life Story I Will Write One Day, Saleable Articles Ideas (I've accumulated over 8,000 without any special effort to do so), Janitorial Humour, etc.

Ring-binders are cheap (most of my binders are scrounged 'recycles') and simple to use, and you can assemble a useful library of your very own just in your spare time and odd moments.

I use an inexpensive rubber stamp to stamp my name on all my file materials — and I don't loan files! In seconds I can find anything I have and use it.

School papers and projects

After investing an incalculable amount of love, effort and emotion, not to mention money, to launch our children on the world, we seek evidence to assure ourselves they are going to be productive people. The first trickle of assurance comes in the form of some scribbled art done in playschool and we snatch it into scrapbook storage. By about seven we actually see intelligent words (even if the letters are a little out of alignment); we collect every sheet. In the junior school sentences overcrowd the scrapbook and stuff the drawer. By the time our children leave secondary school, we have mountains and foothills of evidence that our offspring indeed are literate. Once *we're* satisfied our kids have made it, we still can't get rid of the stuff because surely our children's children will want to see how their parents did — so we keep their school work for the grandchildren.

Don't try to keep everything — just enough for a decent sample — and store the ones you save in a folder.

Newspapers

A newspaper is an important tool of communication in our lives; it is also one of the most common forms of litter and clutter in our homes, offices, streets and public buildings. As soon as a newspaper is read (and maybe an article or two torn out), it is obsolete. Yet the average person keeps a week's (or a month's or...) papers around in case he might want to go back and reread them. Who has ever read a newspaper twice? But once you set one down or tuck it away, the chances of discarding it are infinitesimal.

The bad news is that there is no magic

formula for stopping newspapers becoming one of your biggest, most consistent clutter headaches. Newspapers are as dependable as the dawn. If you fall behind in reading them, they will be there in an enormous pile waiting; if you finish reading them, they will be there in an enormous pile waiting to be disposed of. The uses for which old newspapers work *best* are few — counting all the bird-cage bottoms, painting jobs, moving or packing wadding, window cleaning (ugh), dog training and slow-burning papier mâché fires — only about .001 per cent of newspapers are used after reading.

There are only two ways to handle newspapers. One is instant disposal — the moment you have finished reading them. The other is the faithful paper collection. Scouts, Guides, play-groups, schools and many other organizations in your area are probably still collecting newspaper to sell to a recycling company. Tie them up in bundles and let these people have them regularly — so they don't amass in your garage and crowd you out.

Office clutter

The words 'shop', 'industrial' and 'office' offer a great (but invalid) sanctuary for junk. Somehow we feel we can get by with piles of rubbish if it is hidden away 'at work'. But don't kid yourself: offices are among some of the worst junk stores ever. Hidden away in desks, gathering dust in filing cabinets and coat and cleaning cupboards are massive amounts of clutter.

In twenty-five years of cleaning and inspecting some of the largest and most elite office complexes, I've found that a high percentage of cleaning, breakage, fire and injury costs result from plain unnecessary clutter. Boxes of outdated files and discontinued printing are everywhere, stacked to dangerous heights, inviting toppling and lifting injuries. Extra pencils, pads, pens, clips and organizer trays are generally overdone by at least fifty per cent. On tops of desks and cabinets you'll find department store displays of ungodly excess: ashtrays, trophies, commemorative paperweights, cartoons, centrefolds, elaborate nameplates and pen sets, ceremonial letter openers, mouldy coffee cups and outdated paperwork. Though fancy pen sets come in every design and material imaginable, I've never found any that write much better than a 20p Bic. Few of us like to carry good pens because the carried pen/pencil mortality rate is about sixty per cent. If we don't lose it, some absent-minded person like me innocently walks off with it. So I have many gold gift sets that I shuffle and dust, waiting for the day that I'll write a book in public view. Meanwhile, they're crammed away, jamming my drawers every time I open or close them.

Office junk includes unnecessary furniture, too, because of the unwritten office rule that you never surrender any item of furniture once you get it — whether you need it or not.

Most office stationery cupboards are blessed with rolls or boxes of fresh new labels, business cards or letterheads with outdated or misspelled or slightly misprinted addresses. Keeping them in the hope of having a 50p-an-hour kid go through and revise them with a rubber stamp will never happen — and if they stay around, one day a new office employee will find and use them, with some resulting very sad situations.

And why can't we throw out obsolete or disintegrating rubber stamps? It seems that once a name or message is engraved in rubber on the bottom of a wooden block, it's engraved in our very souls. I found thirty in an old desk I bought, and kept them for years because they cost £5 each now and after all they *did* print. Finally, realizing I'd never use them (I couldn't update their 1940s message to the 1980s), I threw them out.

Every office has its catacombs of clutter, even a professional cleaning firm like mine (here comes another confession). As our business grew, we kept up with the new furniture, forms and equipment we needed. About twelve years ago, to expedite matters further, we made what we considered a wise purchase and bought two large full-key electric adding machines. You could punch in anything, hit the total button, and those things would snort, whirl and click out the most impressive rhythms of taps and grinds you ever heard, finally spitting out a tape of the transaction — we thought we had Einstein encased in plastic!

Two months later I was in a friend's office and he showed me a new fangled electronic calculator, a tiny thing that did twice as much as mine in less than half the time and cost a quarter as much. I thought it was a hoax but of course it wasn't — those amazing, accurate, efficient and low-priced midgets have since taken over.

And today my two big ugly electric adding machines, still brand new, sit under the dust and cobwebs in our stationery cupboard, poised for the day the cunning calculator might fail and they can be re-enlisted. That day will never come. Those adding machines are as worthless as the four chairs with armrests and two casters missing, those balding blotters, the original 1953 copying machine, the hole-puncher we used three times in five years, the stapler that jammed as óften as it stapled, the box of green typewriter ribbon somebody thought would be a nice change and the 1979 calendar note pads waiting to be made into scrap paper. I'll cast my clutter out, if you'll cast out yours.

Business before treasure

Fancy offices are ego boosters (or a cushy prelude to over-charging!). They have nothing to do with production. In some offices there are more swords, bits of armour, helmets, sheepskins, ships, tapestries, carvings and extra cushions than a Viking could carry out on a good day. Others are so full of oriental rugs, glowering old oil portraits and antique furniture that you're waiting for the hounds and huntsmen to come thundering down the hall. Atmosphere comes more from people than from props — 'image'-strewn offices generally house a person with more than the average share of insecurities. All of this costs money to buy, time to clean and worry to protect.

And when you have to wrestle daily with an elegant, unwieldy phone, or come to terms with the fact that your snazzy revolving address file has spilled its contents all over your desk top, *production* is impaired. When arranging the accessories or discussing the decor won't allow you to concentrate on the problem at hand, *function* is suffering.

Walk into any office and list the visible junk honestly. Now inspect the bottom desk drawers and cabinet storage areas. I bet you'll average fifty per cent junk. If you don't want to go through this clutter now, just wait until you move. You'll see! If you are the junkee, repent. If the employer of the junkee, command and demand de-junking. It'll save a fortune in time — and be a lot safer and better-looking too.

In brief, junk

Filing cabinets, vaults, safes, cellars and portfolios can all house clutter and few will dare question it. But the most sanctified of all official clutter containers is the briefcase. To carry, or even own one, seems to be a milestone in many lives. You can tell the executive stature by the size and style of the case — the slimmer and more refined it is, the more important the character carrying it. Briefcases and all their brethren are now being designed into junk; we have teak attaché cases and elegant leather ones costing up to £500, not to mention snakeskin, sharkskin, stainless steel, brushed aluminium, plastic and cow hide — and to carry what? If you looked in most of them, the only briefs you'd find are some worn underpants.

Briefcases are generally full of things people don't use but are supposed to carry — or things they're *not* supposed to carry. I just looked in mine — I am chairman of a group of companies, a managing director, I sit on several other boards, own and run several businesses — I'm lugging around three A4 pads and two pens that don't work (I must have kept them to clean my ears), a £400 dictaphone I've used once in five years (though I did entertain my grandchildren with it once), lapel pins, toilet keychains, squeegee tie pins, a harmonica, guitar pick, my Boy Scout badges, three projects I'm meaning to do and . . . well, never mind, it's too embarrassing.

No clutter is excused by its container!

Could a book be junk?

We all have a certain awe for a book, almost regardless of the contents. A book seems to be an entity or institution in its own right. Maybe because we know how long it takes to write and publish a book; maybe because our parents or grandparents had only a few books and kept them forever. Or maybe because we associate books with the positives of education, knowledge and wisdom. Once that mass of paper, regardless of what it says or shows, is bound and given a title we feel it's sacred.

Recently I had a grand book burning spree. These are some of the titles I cremated.

The first was a 1929 typewriting book, yellow and brittle with age. Then there was *Modern Taxation Moves for a Small Business* (1951), a 1928 book of modern classroom accounting, a guide to gear ratio adjustment on the modern tractor (1934), a turn-of-the-century guide to irrigation systems, a 1947 almanac, *Current Used Car Prices 1963*, a 1971 college prospectus, a map of camp-sites from the late '50s (I knew this was useless when I ended up camping in a shopping mall), a road atlas from the Pleistocene era, a *Political Geography of the World 1937* and eleven boxes of other beautiful books that had absolutely no value to me or anyone else. They contained outdated, incomplete or inaccurate information, but they were books!

Honesty and my library

And why do we amass and keep these piles of books? An impressive case of books

is considered a must when planning a sitting room. Those books are seldom opened; they just sit and gleam and multiply and give an intellectual air to the room they adorn, or serve as a reminder to the children, visitors and relatives that we have scholastic and educational wisdom in our home.

Do even businessmen need to lay out vast sums of money to equip themselves with books on company law and tax guidance? No, because in the fast-moving business climate and fluctuations of the economy, those books are almost worthless a year after they're bought. When we need an answer, we can get it current and accurate in four minutes from a banker or accountant.

We've all heard of the handsomely bound volumes bought by the foot to lend an air of gravity to the board room, but have you ever met the ones which are glued together en bloc? I kid you not! This must be the epitome of book vanity.

De-junk your bookshelf

There is no sacredness to books any more: TV, radio and other media present 'live' material we once had to read.

Books today are produced cheaply and printed on large presses that can roll out ten thousand books in a few hours. Most books today are not beautiful and they're not made to last as they once were. Many books today are not painstakingly compiled wisdom or information but essentially entertainment. Once the majority of books were educational, uplifting, edifying; now many are strictly for profit — anything that will sell will be written and published. Books in short, are not the special repositories of distilled knowledge they once were.

Yes, there are still books today that are sturdy, beneficial and better than the old. I can't and don't want to pass judgement on your books but honestly, how many of them would you read if you were trapped with them on a desert island?

Even cookery books can be clutter

Two of the biggest-selling types of book on the market today are cookery books and diet/exercise books. Guess how many are kept: all of them. How many are used? Few. If and when a cookery book is taken off the shelf it is usually just for a few recipes in the entire book. And though a book might be worth buying for one or two items, the other 372 pages of exotic dishes are junk. Most cooks use a handful of recipe cards (or the recipe on the box or package) for their favourite stand-bys, but *all* keep drawers or cupboards full of cookery books.

Now then, be strict with yourself! Cookery books may make you *feel* domestic, but do you ever use them for cooking? Why not cut out the few recipes you need and meet me at the bonfire.

You don't have to own a book to read it. Try using your local library. Buy to keep only the books you *know* you'll read and

re-read. Or buy a paperback at £3.95 and chuck it out or pass it on when you've read it.

P.S. When de-cluttering, don't forget to look through your 'mini-books', too: for outdated government publications and old maps and guidebooks and pamphlets and brochures, instruction booklets to appliances you no longer have, old phone books, instructions for crafts you've given up, etc. And don't be so eager to *add* booklets to your shelves (and suitcases). Are you really every going to want to read the guidebook to the Chedder Gorge again?

Snapshot clutter

The only value a photo has is in being seen.

Even good and worthwhile things can evolve into junk and clutter your life and environment. A prime example is photographs. What a priceless property our own pictures can be — they allow us to relive precious moments, stimulate memories, bring laughter and warmth to our families, friends and workmates. But if you're like most people, probably seventy-five per cent of your pictures are stacked away, boxed, buried, bent or unfindable.

Hence these expensive, potentially stimulating, heart-warming items are junk, to you. For years this has been the case, yet we continue to take more pictures and slides, show them for a while when they're fresh, then throw them in a drawer, box or pile, thinking, 'One day I'll. . . ' But we never do.

Well, take the bull by the horns and sort these photos now. Here are some tips to help you.

1. Create categories that fit *you*, such as:
Family; Friends; Holidays; Special occasions and events; Other categories.

2. Eliminate bad or unwanted pictures
Throw away. Include here all bad shots — unless they're the only one you have of your great aunt Sarah.
Give away. You may have lots of pictures that have little or no value to you, but may be of interest to people in them. Give or post them to people who might want them.

3. Sort all the remaining pictures into the categories they fit
You'll probably find youself adding or changing a few categories as you go. At this stage identify all faces and places while you remember who they are.

4. Now decide on the best way to display your pictures.

Prints
These can be mounted in sturdy, durable albums — there are lots of different types to choose from.

I like the ring-binder albums with looseleaf plastic pocket pages. These are inviting to use and practically indestructible. The prints are nicely displayed (and the pages can be handled safely even by little children, who get the most out of pictures).

Or you could display them mounted on the wall, it doesn't have to be expensive or difficult. There are shops which will do it. True, they charge, but there are DIY kits too. Also you can buy frames quite cheaply at Woolworths in which you can mount and hang your pictures. As a cleaner, I really like things hung instead of placed (on pianos, etc.). If you have to move Grandpa every time you clean or dust, you grow to dislike him!

Negatives should be stored in manilla envelopes in a handy file so you can get at them easily to have copies made for the friends and family who want them.

Slides
Slide trays are tidy and really worth the money. They simplify not only storage but use. I like the standard 140-slide tray; it's easy to store, use and add to. In slide trays your pictures will be permanently organized to look at again and again. Label the tray with the category or identification. These slide boxes can be stored in, on, or under anything and still be usable in seconds.

You can even make your own cassette — voice or music — to play with some of the trays.

Chapter 9

Dress less for success

In the Dark Ages an excess of wearing apparel was justified by the need for *protection*; today our excess of wearing apparel is justified by the word *fashion*. That magic word keeps the factories and looms of the world rolling by making sure, with bi-annual changes of style, that things keep coming in and going out.

Fashion lurches from flares and stack soles to drainpipes and sloppy pumps. One season leather and silk are all the rage, the next tweed and knits.

We buy it all — and if we manage to resist, our offspring, cousins and friends buy it for us. Somehow we gather and keep all these clothes, packing them tighter and tighter in our ever larger cupboards and wardrobes with no hope of ever wearing them out. How many ties or scarves or, for that matter, suits have you owned that ever wore out? Style is an even greater cause of waste than greed is.

Fashion seduces intelligent human beings into paying ridiculous prices for clothing that makes them all look the same. The word 'wardrobe' convinces others that they need platoons of shoes,

racks of dresses, squadrons of suits, shirts and blouses.

While most of us stand by like a bunch of mute models, somebody out there is piling clothes on us unmercifully. They are fiddling around with our hemline, neckline, bustline, waistline — and most of all, our credit line. And when they can't alter the style any more, they change the colours by the year, and then the season.

Did you know you have a small fortune sunk in your wardrobe? You sincerely tried to dress for success and ended up with a cupboard full of clutter. Now let's try dressing *less* for success. Throw some of it out (you want to, anyway). Clothes clutter affects your life in more ways than how hard it is to fit another hanger in the cupboard.

Clothing that is neat, attractive, comfortable, wears well, protects us and helps us project our feelings and physical self is a worthy investment. It's the clothes that over-decorate us, strain our personality and our wallet that are clutter.

Most of us don't need clothes to take

over for us. When you consider the power of the eyes, facial expression, voice and body movement in the sum total of what makes a person 'attractive', anything else seems insignificant. Yet we hang incredible arrays of fabrics and leathers (and if we can afford it, precious metals and stones) on ourselves. Draped over or fastened onto our bodies, they take hours and hours of our lives, not only to pay for, but to wear and care for.

I've seen people dressed up in such elaborate material they look more like the living room curtains than a living person. Others are in clothes so styled, tailored and tight, they can't sit, run or breathe deeply (though they can stand and rotate).

Why should we clog our wardrobes with things we rarely or never wear, that don't keep us warm or cool or dry when we need to be, and don't even permit any comfortable movement?

Take a long, hard look at your wardrobe and avoid stockpiling clothes which are a nuisance to launder and iron, are way outdated, or were foolish buys.

Be careful with clothes you have to be careful with

Many people praise my wife because no matter where, when or what the call for her help, she can be out of the door in a minute for any emergency or for a three week trip. The secret of her quickness I think, has a lot to do with her wardrobe.

One birthday I offered her a beautiful fur coat — she turned me down! Her logic for the decision was excellent: 'I'd have to be very careful with a fur coat. There aren't that many place I could really go in it and even then I couldn't sit in it because the back would wear out. Knowing it was so expensive, it'd be hard to relax in it and I'd have to worry about it being stolen. I'd

have to avoid Sue and John, two friends who are allergic to fur. The grandchildren's dribbles would ruin it and I'd have to keep it in a special place in the cupboard, have to put it in cold storage and insure it and mothproof it and even worry about looking ostentatious.' It wouldn't be worth the things she'd have to sacrifice for it.

My wife believes in clothes that are easy to launder and stay looking neat and pressed. This makes sense if you think about the cost of maintaining awkward fabrics.

What about those suits and skirts and trousers that only look good for the first half hour you wear them, and then sag and wrinkle and crease and embarrass you for the rest of the day. . .those blouses and shirts that will never look good without dampening and starching and a good twenty minutes bent over the ironing board (a twenty minutes you're never willing to spend). . . those flimsy things and special fabrics that have to be taken to the dry cleaner after *every* wearing (how many times the price of the garment will you end up paying in 'maintenance' fees?).

Unadmitted 'obsoletes'

Most of us have a small universe of things inhabiting our clothes cupboard that we've outgrown, physically and mentally, or that are just unusable, but we haven't got round to admitting it yet. These are among the prime contributors to cupboard over-crowding, and can actually be rather easily de-junked if we force ourselves to have a good blitz.

There are not many wardrobes around which do not have at least some sweet little dresses that were *very* becoming on us (fifteen years ago), that have sat in their plastic bags for the last ten years (and will for the *next* ten) ugly old coats and bedraggled beloved dressing gowns, ties that are out of style (or in style but we don't like them anyway), clothes that shrank or got scorched (but we couldn't face throwing them away at the moment of trauma), stretched polo necks, broken necklaces, disintegrating bras, mateless gloves, more 'shirts and trousers to wear when I'm painting' than a lifetime of decorating will ever require, tights in colours we'll *never* want our legs to be, jumpsuits we always admire but keep passing over when it comes to choosing something to actually wear.

Impulse clothes

The clothes we wear the least are often the ones we bought the fastest. We really didn't need or want them, but the mood of the moment mesmerized us. We've all lugged home clogs from Holland, mantillas from Spain, shapeless dresses with the Greek key pattern on from Greece. We snap up commemorative T-shirts that instantly become outdated and return from the seaside laden with embarrassing and unwearable bits of clothing.

Costumery / quaint / outrageous / gift clothing often falls into this category, too. Your wife *might* look great in that red satin Chinese dress slit to the waist, those rainbow-striped harem pants or rhinestone-studded boots — but would she be caught dead in them? It's sometimes a nice idea to give gifts your loved ones would never indulge themselves in, but don't let your impulses and fantasies override their self-image — you might end up making them feel uncomfortable and guilty, in addition to junking up their lives.

Unused impulse clothes are among our most conspicuous clutter. Go to your wardrobe now. Pick out all your impulse clothes. Don't ask yourself 'Why did I do it?' We're all weak. Ask yourself, 'Why do I *keep* it?' Then you know what to do.

Whittle down your wardrobe

Subject every article of clothing in your cupboard to these close scrutinies.

1. If it's not flattering to you — the colour or the cut is wrong — pull it out.

2. If it doesn't fit or it's not comfortable — you have to pull in your stomach, you can't bend over or move your arms, or it's itchy — pull it out.

3. If it's too complicated — if you have to wrap or tuck or tie it just so, or if you have to remember to straighten the sash or pull the bodice up every ten minutes, pull it out.

4. If it's too delicate — if you can only wear it where there won't be food or drink or animals or children, where it won't be too hot because you don't want to sweat in it or too cold because a coat or jacket will crease it — pull it out.

5. If it's badly damaged or has an important part missing that you probably won't be able to replace — pull it out.

6. If it needs to be altered or repaired before you can wear it — pull it out.

7. If you never or very rarely wear it (because your lifestyle has changed or it just isn't called for more than once a half-century), or if you can only wear it with certain things (that you don't have or really don't like wearing) — pull it out.

Leave in the cupboard everything you wear consistently and feel good in; and make two piles of all the rest.

Pile One
Needs to be cleaned or repaired — there's some practical reason why you're not wearing it.

Pile Two
Is out of style or doesn't fit or you've decided you just don't want to be bothered with it any more.

Pile One — clean or mend (several of these pieces, when you look at them closely, will join Pile Two). Arrange what's left in the cupboard according to colour coordination and needs. (And when you see something in a sale, think about how it will fit in with your basic wardrobe and how *often* you'll wear it — not just how much you'll save).

There are many places where Pile Two could be gratefully received. Charity shops like Oxfam are especially keen to receive expensive cast offs like good coats, suits and evening wear which they can sell. Oxfam also runs a clothes collection for the needy in the Third World. Really way out stuff might be welcome at playgroups and nurseries as dressing ups. Out of fashion shirts make good painting overalls for small children. Or, if you have a lot of good stuff why not think of selling it? There is a rash of nearly-new second-hand shops around nowadays. Better a pound in the pocket than a load of moth-gathering garments in the cupboard.

Down at the heels: junk

No more astonishing proof of human devotion to style at the expense of utility exits than in the case of our footwear.

Shoes down there on the grubby ground house our far-from-delightful feet and are necessary to protect them. People possess shoes by the pile, many never worn more than a few times. People buying shoes stalk, parade, twist, rotate and jig in front of shoe shop mirrors for an unbelievable length of time — not concerned with comfort or durability, but with how they'll look to others.

The lowly shoe is responsible for a lot of physical torture, too. The vast majority of shoe styles — men's and women's — are somewhere between uncomfortable and painful to wear. Trying to explain why a woman would willingly subject her feet to a 4-inch spike heel — so she can't walk, but must wobble and hobble and lurch around — would boggle the finest mind.

Even being a conservative in the shoe style parade, I slid around in sleek slip-ons for fifteen years, because they matched — not my feet, mind you, but the other ridiculous apparel some rich designer designed. Even so, it was hard to buy a shoe I didn't have to snip the bells, buckles and beads off so I could wear it discreetly. Some near-falls on stage and during TV appearances inspired me to look for a sturdier, more practical shoe. I bought a pair of plain old clodhoppers — my feet thought they'd been resurrected. I de-junked all my 'sophisticated' shoes, realizing it was better to plop a little than flop a lot.

How you dress your feet is probably more important to your spirits and physical well-being than anything else you wear. If your feet hurt at the end of the day, or after the first hour, it's time to retread your shoe wardrobe. Comfortable shoes are available for every occasion; it's worth some time, money and trouble now to invest in a few basic pairs of sensible shoes. And throw out (or give away) all those pairs you aren't using. You'll have more room in your cupboard — and you'll be able to stride down the street, skip up the stairs and whistle past the corn pad display.

And all the trimmings

I heard a jeweller remark once in a conference speech that when some men achieve 'success' they buy big cars and nice homes. If they already have these they buy their wives a giant diamond to flaunt their money. It's not for the benefit of the wife, you understand, but for *him* — he's just using her to advertise, so people will say, 'Gosh, Harry is certainly successful, look at that diamond his wife has.' Precious stones can be a good investment, but there are better ones — especially if all you're doing is feeding your ego. Jewellery has to be guarded, insured, duplicated, matched and serviced — it often puts more worry than joy into our lives.

Think about your jewellery — your baubles, bangles, beads and bracelets. If you have to take them off when you wash your hands or are trying to work on something, hide them before you leave home, hide them while you're travelling and hide them in a bank deposit box the rest of the time, maybe it isn't worth it. It's just another thing to worry about and take care of.

And besides — what woman or man really believes that a flashy object dangling from ears or neck enhances personal appeal? What is it that people want most from each other? Warmth, affection, love and feeling. What does £1,000 worth of goldsmith's and silversmith's art do for the heart? People wear more jewellery to impress than to attract in actual fact.

The most beautiful jewellery is usually utterly simple and expresses something meaningful; a mass of gaudy stones draped in six strands of chains is a great place to start de-junking.

Don't persuade yourself that you ought to have rings for this and rings for that. Know yourself and please yourself — don't worry about satisfying society's 'supposed to', 'ought to' traditions, styles and fads. Most of it will end up as junk to you.

Your crowning clutter?

Amazingly enough, some of our clutter is literally 'home grown'.

Anything hairy has caught our fancy in recent years. Hair gets more attention, care, coddling, consulting (and chemicals) than any other part of the body. People will let their lungs, heart, stomach, eyes stand last in line for expenditure — hair rates the number one slot. We spend millions of pounds and hours of time daily tending it, displaying it, repairing it, enhancing it. We nurture face and head hair to the abundance and extent that we have to hire artists to groom it for us.

Yes, it's been called the 'crowning glory' but like anything too complicated, hair can be clutter. Nice clean hair, flowing or curled, *is* attractive, but when it takes more from us than it gives, it begins to dictate our existence. It's sad indeed when fear for our hair stops us swimming, keeps us out of wind and breezes and sun and morning dew, robs us of sleep (those cursed curlers), rules out warm hats, determines what we will do when, causes constant compulsive mirror checking. Hair care for many has become so dominant that our daily routine revolves around 'hair time'.

It's incredible how the output of an epidermal gland has somehow become the ultimate expression of our masculinity or femininity. Do you *really* feel your hair's worth an hour of your time a day or £30 a month to maintain, not to mention storing and ploughing through all the tools to groom it (or the devastation all that fussing inflicts on once-healthy hair and scalp)? Adopting a sane and simple hair style is an easy way to de-junk.

Boot your baggage!

Once we've de-junked what we wear, we'll want to do the same for what we carry. Wallets, handbags and bags are stuffed with clutter, necessitating a sorting exercise every time we need something.

No wonder people fumble. You're in a queue and the customer just ahead of you, completing his or her transaction, reaches into wallet, pocket or purse for money, chequebook, credit card, keys. . . and can't find it. Out comes every imaginable piece of junk. The fumbler can't find what he needs and frantically begins to throw

79

things around and rummage through every pocket and personal carrying space while the other people in the queue begin to mutter at the hold up.

Do you really want to be muttered about? When you find yourself throwing an extra comb in your handbag because you know your chances of finding the other one in there are slim, that's a clear signal that it's time to streamline the stuff you carry.

Lugging too much around with you can actually be dangerous. A young woman from London told me she had carried an 'assailant protection' whistle in her handbag for years, and one dark night when she was pursued — you've guessed it — there was so much clutter in her handbag she couldn't find the whistle. Fortunately, the would-be assailant, intrigued by her rummaging, tapped his toes at a distance for a while, then left.

Clutter is not a credit to you

Among the real prestige clutter is the credit card collection. People love to open their wallets and purses and fan out a cache of credit cards capable of purchasing anything from a shrimp cocktail to a whole canning factory — account cards, cash and carry cards, cheque cards, credit cards, charge-everything cards, card protection cards — twenty, thirty, even more cards. All this demonstrates, of course, that they have .fabulous credit (or are poor managers and have to pay for everything in instalments). Extra or unnecessary cards are junk, *plastic junk*. You don't need all of them; if you lose your wallet or purse your risk is compounded twenty times, besides which they are awkward to carry around. When I decided my clutter was killing me, my string of credit cards went; for ten years now I've carried only two — and I've travelled the world over, bought dinners, lodging, petrol, tickets, supplies, gifts and never (even once) needed any more. It was one of the most delightful de-junking moves I ever made — try it! Plus you'll pay fewer interest charges and spend less money on unnecessary things that were easy to buy with all those cards that made you think you were rich.

Chapter 10

Junk on wheels

Because we all spend so much time in the confines of our cars they carry some of the finest clutter collections in the world. When we leave the car and go inside the house, we feel our junk is safe in a sealed vault. So we can ignore those disposable nappies fermenting under the front seat, the empty bottles rolling on the floor, the pips and dried peels, decomposing apple cores, broken side lights, thermostats and mirrors, the map of the Lake District stained with sour milk ('We might go again, after all, it's been five years'). Even the key ring is so heavy it turns off the engine on its own. It's filled with the sacred collection of Grandma's house keys, the keys to the broken lock on the garden shed, the bicycle lock, the office keys, the key to the car sold four months ago, a miniature (non-working) torch, and a magnifying glass with a screwdriver in the handle. Some cars in their final year of clutter accumulation could be promoted to refuse lorries.

Cars were never meant to be four-wheeled files for old parking stickers and unpaid fines, antique gas bill receipts, peanut shells, drink cans, crushed fast food containers and tissue boxes, sweet wrappers, directions to past parties, single-lensed sunglasses, flattened matchboxes, dried-out first-aid kits and non-fitting fuses. These things are junk — why carry them around?

The junk problem in vehicles escalated when motor homes/caravans came out. Like homes in miniature they have all the same junk hazards, including the literal kitchen sink that attracts dozens of itsy-bitsy little accessories, from spice racks and scouring pad holders to elaborate utensil collections: ham slicers, cheese cutters, garlic presses, pastry crimpers.

One car can create more junk than forty kids rummaging through neighbours' piles of rubbish. Every vehicle somehow manages to sprout a bumper crop of extra rims, hubcaps, jacks and yes, even those insect-spattered and gravel-dented old licence plates. You finally sell the beast or drag it off to the junkyard, but the shrapnel of its demise remains behind — dispersed into every corner of the garage, attic, basement and tool box. Certain that no one else would properly value the treasure that decorates your trusted vehicle, you take hours to strip it of the transfers, stickers, waving hands, fuzzy dice, deodorant strips, broken scrapers, monogrammed floor mats, back seat clothes hangers, and, as a last act, scoop up the oil change stickers on the doorframe.

The epitome of car junkdom is keeping the whole car when it expires — people often do this when it's too far gone to trade in. They feel they owe old Betsy a decent home or, eventually, burial. Now, when a hungry car dealer won't even give us a trade in, that's a pretty strong hint that what we have has moved beyond clutter, to *menace*. But we tow the banger home and park it. The tyres go flat, birds use it for a target range, the sun bleaches the upholstery and cracks the dash board, the windows get broken mysteriously, friends scavenge parts, our teenage son backs into it twice with the new car, our neighbour's child squashes his tiny finger in the door, a cat has kittens on the back seat. The bonnet, wide open like a begging alligator, matches the sprung-latched boot. The old car is totally shamed and demoralized, but illusions of antiquity now cloud our judgement — we keep it. When at last, after years more cannibalizing, divorce is threatened unless we do get rid of the unsightly heap, we take it to the local breaker's yard.

If a car won't go or isn't used, why keep it in the first place? It's taking space and cluttering up your drive. Unless you're restoring an old classic for a hobby or using a banger to teach your children car care and hard work it can clutter your life. What is your opinion of people who turn their cars into tips?

Few things are more revolting than a cluttered car. When we see a messy vehicle we have a tendency to treat the owner as slouchily as he treats the car. And a seedy front seat tends to be a sign of an untidy house or flat — have you noticed how copiously crudded cars and sadly messy dwellings seem to go hand in hand?

The (wrong) car in every garage

Many people make poor decisions when buying a car. A large camper is impractical for an average retired couple, a velvet-seated Carlton is not the right transport for a shepherd with four dogs and a sick sheep forever in tow, a slick two-door sports model is not the smartest way to haul four children to Guide camp (though a nice tough estate might be).

When you get a vehicle for show or ego, it usually ends up junking up your life — it doesn't serve your needs and you don't get the full benefit of what it *does* have to offer. And affordability isn't only a question of economics — many rich people can't emotionally afford the vehicle junk they have.

The pleasure of driving a fine machine isn't the main reason most people own a glamorous petrol guzzler — they often only want to own one as a status symbol.

Paying extra for safety or comfort — maybe even power — on your vehicle might make sense, but most 'extras' sooner or later become junk to you.

How often have we seen a family struggling — a young wife with several children, rarely able to pay the bills and keep the children clothed — while the husband has to play the macho man with a giant souped-up nobby-tyred pick-up or an impractical sports car loaded with

extras simply to enhance his image.

Car sales (and prices) soar when the manufacturer adds 'CIT', 'XR' or 'Sport' on a strip of plastic chrome. The reason dealers display their prestige line in the showroom is to get men (who are far weaker than women when it comes to cars) to come in and look and imagine themselves careering past crowds of admiring onlookers as they manoeuvre this magnificent, powerful machine through life.

A car is merely a mode of transport, yet it has been designed and marketed as a •status symbol, personality outlet, aggression releaser and pacifier. People spend almost twice as much as they need to on a car and boast or talk about it more than about family, friends or personal health.

People can easily find hours to wash, polish and pamper a car, yet can't find minutes to brush their teeth. They can make a staggering payment on a car, or spend £5,000 or more on a prestige model, yet not be able to afford a weekly long-distance call to Mum or Dad or a £2 donation to the Girl Guides.

They will know every engineering wonder and specification of that special model and not even know their nieces'

and nephews' birthdays, or what time to be at work. Do you want to spend all that emotional, spiritual and physical strength on sustaining a *possession?*

Maybe it's not time for a trade in

One day a friend of mine mentioned that since he'd been married (he has seven children, three of them now in college) he'd spent a total of only £13,000 on cars (and he's always driven a safe, handsome, fully-paid-for vehicle around). That didn't seem possible to me because for some time now those nice cars have been costing £9,000-£15,000 each. His simple secret (and one I now follow) is to wait a year or two, watch the paper and buy a nice clean, sound £10,000 used car for £3,500 direct from a first owner or from a dealer — and then keep it maintained and de-junked. It lasts many years and will usually be running well enough to pass on to his children, who drive it for another five years.

I went back and reviewed the cars (business and personal) I'd owned since 1957 (sixty of them), and almost every one, once I sold or traded it in, was run for years by the next owner and more years by the one after that. I imagined the new owners must have rebuilt them entirely, but not so — they just replaced a belt and gasket.or two and cranked'er up. Once I bought a '54 Ford Ten truck with 70,000 miles on it, beat it up hauling cleaning gear for five years, and put another 70,000 miles on it. I reckoned it must have had it (the battery was weakening) and sold it to my neighbour for £25. He replaced the battery, mended the door handles and drove it for five more years. It finally got so ugly he decided it had really had it, and sold it to a student. One day three years later, when I was doing my Christmas shopping in a town many miles away, I saw the old '54 Ford, same dents, my faded Contractors logo still adorning the doors, parked with the Jaguars and Range Rovers. A lad came out of the shopping precinct, jumped in and drove off, smooth as silk!

When I sat down and thought about it, the reason I got rid of cars was usually that a catch was broken, the clock had stopped working, the glove compartment light went out, a window stuck or there was a tear in the upholstery.

Don't do it! It's a poor investment. Sit down and calculate your vehicle purchase and running costs for the last ten or twenty years. Now work out what you could have done with that amount of money if you'd followed a more practical course.

The adjustment to a whole new way of thinking is a difficult one, but it will pay you some amazing dividends. I wasn't at all sure I should keep driving a vehicle when it reached the 100,000 or 125,000 mark. I could scarcely believe it was still running well, and pictured myself driving somewhere and the whole motor or transmission suddenly disintegrating or dropping out on the road — but that nightmare never comes true. I was just being seduced by the new-car enchantress.

Yes, I do have a little repair problem now and again, but the glory of no payments, low insurance premiums and all the other nice paid-for goodies more than make up for it.

Since I kicked the expensive habit of

mobile mothballing, I've been constantly reassured it was the best move I've made — cars don't wear out as fast as our resistance to new models. Cars don't drive me, I drive them and I love it. Your car can go to 100,000 miles — if you're careful!

When adding subtracts...

Some of the best designers, engineers and decorators in the world work for manufacturers, expending great research and effort on making cars efficient and beautiful. They work for years to achieve precision and balance in a model's power, mechanics, size and weight for maximum durability and safety. Yet when ownership falls into our hands our impulse to clutter it up is surpassed only by our urge to redesign it.

We modify pipes for more noise, jack up or weigh down the frame, reshape the grille, install miniature traffic lights in the rear window, add larger tyres, bigger carburretors and a horn that plays bugle calls.

Car stickers

Most are junk. Possible exceptions are those which announce to the drivers behind that you slow down for horses or that you carry children in the back seat. But what can 'Honk if you had it last night' possibly be but distracting? This goes for all those dangling furry dice, nodding dogs and fairy brake lights that some of us decorate our vehicles with. Even cassette players can be dangerous. The moment we're fiddling with the tapes could be the fatal one.

For a clutter-free vehicle:

1. Keep a rubbish bin in the garage or driveway. This will make it easy and convenient to throw rubbish away when you're getting in or out of the car.

2. Make sure you have any necessary tools, jacks, shovels, chains, etc., in a sturdy box in your boot. Better still, roll them up in a blanket. This keeps tools compact, quiet, and provides a nice mat if you need to crawl under or over the car.

3. Keep some small plastic bin liners handy and as bits of food and other rubbish builds up on a trip, put it in the bag immediately. Smells and stains that mess up cars usually result from *left over* food, not from the act of eating itself.

4. Carry a J cloth (See *Is There Life After Housework?*) in the glove compartment. It will pick up the dust effectively. I also carry a spray bottle of alcohol-based window cleaner and a cloth in the boot for spills, mud on lights and other cleaning needs.

5. Don't screw, bolt or glue cheap accessories and gadgets all over the vehicle.

6. Clean and wash the *inside* of the car occasionally, too. A wet/dry vacuum and a handy brush will clean seats and floor mats easily.

Modern transport offers us tremendous advantages and conveniences. But a vehicle is not an extra house, room, shed or mobile dining car. It isn't a trophy wall, moving van or a six-cylinder hoarding. *It is transport!* One of the biggest destroyers of human life today is the car used for things other than reasonable transport.

Drive de-junked. The skin and sanity you save will be your own.

Chapter 11

Junk danger zones

There are some places we have to frequent less or avoid altogether if we intend ever to be cured of junkosis.

Frequenting shopping precincts (plazas, squares, centres, complexes or any of their other aliases) is suicide: even an innocent amble through will insinuate something you don't really need in to your shopping bag. Never go to such places if you don't need anything.

Next time you go to a shopping precinct, before you buy or look at anything, sit down on a bench and watch the customers. You'll notice the majority of them shuffling along purposelessly, often not after anything in particular, just looking for what they *might* need. The displays, decor and smell of the precinct seem to have a hypnotic hold, and you'll see people just wandering up and down the arcades looking for action.

The media — and perhaps our parents, teachers and friends — have inadvertently taught us that happiness comes from things: that's why when we feel 'down' or depressed and want a lift we often want to buy something. That's why

people wander aimlessly through shopping centres and gift shops — they don't even know *what* they want. They just crave the experience of buying a new thing every so often. The minute they buy it, the time starts ticking away till the next time they have to do that. And when they do get something, it just triggers the urge for the next and next — all of which compounds accumulation. Just picking up 'one little thing' here and 'one little thing' there is where the pile of clutter came from.

'Recreational' shopping is a mistake. If you need, want or have to have a specifc something, go and get it, but just poking around a shop (or anywhere there is a glamorous array of goods, food or whatever) is a temptation you don't need. It will seduce you into acquiring things that will needlessly clutter your life.

The languid locations

Some locations are particularly perilous because a high proportion of what they sell is clutter or they actually *specialize* in things that are junk to most of us (scarcely or non-functional, largely decorative, often expensive 'stuff'). Fortunately, we are given a clue to this before we ever enter by the very name of the place.

Any shop with the word *'gift'* in its name.

Ye Olde, etc. when Old is spelled *Olde* ... watch out! (Anything with an extra 'e' on the end is probably a junk dive.)

Anything with an animal in the name: *The Busy Bee, The Bashful Bunny, the Fragrant Frog, The Rumpled Unicorn* ...

Anything that sports an ampersand, or has an *'N'. N' Stuff, N' Things* is a dead giveaway.

Anything that substitutes Ks for Cs: *The Kozy Korner, The Kopper Kettle.*

For that matter, anything with *'Country'* or *'Corner'* in the name.

Trees or plants in names are also suspect: *The Chestnut Tree, The Daisy Chain, The Cedar Cabin.*

Car boot sale sickness

Car boot sales have increased about five hundred per cent in the last decade — the ultimate public confession that the house runneth over, a family fight is inevitable if the junk stays, or they need cash to buy some different things.

These events are particularly dangerous for junkers because there they will be surrounded by dozens of displays of tantalizing junk brought by fellow junkers. Even if they do dispose of all the rubbish they have taken away to the sale, they will, like as not, return with the car

boot stuffed full of a new lot of 'bargains' and 'treasures'.

It's not amazing enough that the junkee pays out perfectly good money for this trash — he or she actually experiences euphoric feelings of cleverness and joy at having scored such a hit. These feelings usually dissipate by the time the victim reaches home, however. Having by now returned to full consciousness and taken a second look at the plunder, the hapless junkee goes into a fit of depression.

If you're serious about saving yourself from junkosis, car boot sales may well be a pleasure you might wish to forgo.

The car boot sale has a few relatives also worth avoiding. The *jumble sale*, for example, is an increasingly rare species that still lingers on in church halls, often heavily inhabited by charming chirping ladies. The jumble sale abounds in shabby but genteel junk — worn books, limp afghans, faded plastic flower arangements and impossible 1960s clothing. The *flea market*, on the other hand, is a vigorous and fast-growing hybrid that springs up in shopping precincts, building sites, back streets and town halls — anywhere there is abundant space for display. Here the innocent is adrift in a sea of separate booths featuring a breathtaking variety of junk — old, middle-aged and even brand spanking new. Velvet paintings, Last Supper rugs, log-slice clocks; hubcaps, novelty booze bottles, comic books, used paperbacks, tattered girlie magazines and printed T-shirts of every description are standard flea market fare. You even stand a good chance of being able to lay your hands on a genuine (£5) wrench for only £6.50.

Some junk danger zones are less widespread than others — not everyone passes through them — but they're no less deadly for being less frequented. If you're due to pass through these areas soon, begin preventative therapy *now*.

Conference clutter

Have you ever watched crowds at a conference as they scoop up all those badges, brochures, booklets, pens, posters, stickers, samples and special-release records — and cart them home? We even save the plastic bags they gave us to carry the clutter in, and our plastic badge holders to remember the glory of our name in lights (or at least felt-tip marker). Maybe one day we'll have enough to slip in new cards and reuse them to run our *own* conference (the annual Junkman's conference?). . . I bet my whole stack of play money those of you who've been to a conference or trade fair within the past year *still* haven't got round to using (or even sorting) the bumf you dragged home. Embarrassing, isn't it?

Passing fancy junk

When any type of craze sweeps the nation, a large percentage of us join in. We buy fast, pay more and almost immediately our enthusiasm fizzles out. Homes and cars are stuffed to the ceiling with seldom used 'good as new' objects, such as:

aquariums
jogging accessories
video games
fondue sets
massaging footbaths
diet books and plans
weights and exercise machines
metal detectors
organs and pianos
stereo headphones
stone polishers

food processors
fad style clothes
movie cameras
weaving looms
yogurt makers
sandwich toasters
egg boilers
macrame kits
wine making equipment
guitars
trampolines
CB radios
walkie-talkies
slow cookers
wood-burning stoves
ice cream makers

Most of this is bought on the spur of the moment and before the new smell has vanished, so has our interest. As costly as it may have been, it's now a burden to us.

Beware the ides of March and February and December and...

If you think avoiding gift shops, shopping centres and even car boot sales alone is enough to keep you safe from junk, you're riding for a fall. When you stop and think about it, we're surrounded by special days that circle and bombard us. Study your calendar.

JANUARY
We insist on starting our year off miserably with too much rich food and drink, stupid hats, streamers, pages of unresolved resolutions and twenty-seven more calendars than we'll ever use.

FEBRUARY
No sooner have we recovered from Christmas, packed the decorations away, thrown the balding Christmas tree into the garden and taken down the cards,

than it's time for another round of card sending. Valentine cards are usually huge, expensive and in extremely bad taste. But we keep them. We keep too the plush, ribboned and lace frilled boxes that the chocolates came in.

APRIL
Easter usually arrives in this month. Think of all the awful Easter egg boxes and broken Easter baskets, battered chicks and bunnies and leftover egg colouring kits that we'll never throw away.

OCTOBER
Halloween has developed into an observed 'festival' over the last ten years. Following in American footsteps we buy masks and witches' hats and make costumes for ghosts, witches and skeletons. We give parties for our children, sometimes for ourselves, and afterwards we store the fancy dress, the ghost glitter, the spare invitation cards and the lanterns.

NOVEMBER
Next comes that most tactless of all celebrations, Guy Fawkes night. Time was when each family let off its own collection of fireworks in their back gardens, strictly on the evening of November 5th. Nowadays the celebrations stretch over a period of ten days or so to accommodate the public displays, the charity shows, the private parties and the individual bonfire nights. Consequently for ten days we're picking up the junk of spent firework cases in parks, gardens and streets. Little plastic parachutes, lodged among the branches of trees, remain there well into next season, an eyesore and an irritation.

DECEMBER

And so to Christmas — a festival unfortunately so far removed from its original spirit that it has become the worst junk generator of the year. We feel bound to shower with presents those who shower us with presents. Feverishly we scour the shops for knick-knacks, curios, oddities, and as the great day draws nearer a mad panic grips us. Almost anything will do as a gift, so long as each person receives a brightly wrapped package from us. What proportion of these gifts become instant junk? And afterwards, of course, we keep the wrapping paper, the glittering string, the cards *and* all the tired old decorations.

For some reason we can't just enjoy the spirit of the day — we have to 'do' it to death. It's as if we have to *prove* we're loving or patriotic or happy or thankful. But the proof is in the feeling, not in the accessories.

Media mania

Every time new heroes come on the TV screen we fall in love with them, but the experience is so passive that to keep our love alive we have to shower ourselves and our shelves with the flood of trinketry that follows. The whole environment is remade in the image of some fictitious creature: T-shirts, notebooks, pencils, perfume, sweets, sleeping bags and sheets and pyjamas, watches, shoes, games, books are everywhere. Can you believe it? We pay for it! £5.95 for a £1.99 T-shirt with some non-existent primordial amphibian silk-screened on the front. It all ends up as junk by the time the next idol takes us.

Celebrity clutter

Don't let the marketing boys dump unwanted junk on you by making you believe that some celebrity uses nothing but their brand. Anyway a guy isn't an authority on what to eat and drink because he took twenty-five wickets at Lords; a woman isn't an ultimate authority on electronics because she stars in domestic comedy in the West End.

Beware of these junk seduction words...

All of us are lambs when it comes to the seductive words and phrases that convince us we can't live through the day without knowing what — feels or tastes like, if we can't own a — of our own. Before soft messages and signs croon you into the arms of Old Mother Junk, make sure you translate them.

Here are some typical words and phrases from the advertisement copy writers' vocabulary to put you on your guard.

Selected	Everything is selected — it could be selected out of the reject pile, the failure file, or the rubbish bin.
Imported	Just about everything is 'imported' from somewhere — how far away doesn't matter much any more.
Premium	Could be a way of marketing something, not an indication of worth or quality.
Limited	They don't say limited to what or where, or how many.
Model	A small imitation of the real thing.
Special	A term of timing — not value! In the right time or circumstances *anything* can be special.

Exclusive	They haven't dared try it anywhere else.
Handmade	A hand touches the tool or mould that makes everything.
Homegrown	Everything is homegrown (even if it's been shipped in from 4,000 miles away).
Free	Law of the Universe: there is nothing without a price.
Revised	It didn't work (or sell) the first time.
Quality	Quality is just a state (it could be good or bad).
Priceless	Smiles are priceless. People are priceless. I've never seen a *thing* that is.
Distinctive	Distinguishable from other things — isn't everything?
Authentic	Genuine junk!
Reduced	Same junk with a different price.
On appro.	Get it now and let it grow on you before you have to pay for it.

The phrase fresheners

Sometimes, no matter how seductively junk is marketed in the first place, it just doesn't sell. So the advertising people are called in to revamp the campaign and they come up with ploys like these.

On Sale	The most desirable things and places don't have to go on sale.
New, Improved	It failed, and we want you to act as guinea-pigs for the second round.
Once-in-a Lifetime	You can be sure that after getting stung this time you'll never do it again.

In style	It's time again to tell people what they like.
For a limited time only	They've only got a few more left to get rid of.
Top-rated	Only means that it's popular — doesn't say why: it could be the only one in town.
Only one per customer	Offer to buy a hundred, they'll love you!
Ten-day trial offer	They can depend on your procrastination.
Not sold in the shops	We decided to hit you direct.
First edition	Is always the worst — mechanically and structurally. All first editions are prototypes, experiments — which means they don't have the bugs worked out yet.
Space age material	Most likely plastic, sometimes called 'space-age technology.'
Years ahead of its time	Just hope it doesn't need a part not invented yet.
Doctors use	Doctors make mistakes and have bad habits, too.
The next best thing to	Please buy this second-best.
No Artificial Preservatives	But surely lots of natural ones.
Factory outlet	No retailer wants it.
First class	Should be the standard, not a degree of excellence.

Two for the price of one	Easiest way to get rid of two pieces of junk simultaneously
Custom-made	The factory made an error.
Order freepost	We'll include the postage in the purchase price.
For Adults only	If you're a twelve-year-old with fuzz on your lip — you're in.
Laboratory-tested	It could have *failed* the test.
Made from selected raw materials	Probably a soup tin you threw away a month ago.
Largest selection available	Nobody else in the area stocks them.
New colours	The same old colours with new names.
Almost too good to believe	It almost fools you every time.
At last, a . . .	It was never really needed.
Order before . . and we'll include. . .	Will you accept a bribe for buying junk?

Everything tagged with these teasers isn't necessarily junk, but how often do we let phrases like these inflate an object's value — and how often do we end up with clutter because of them? You hear people (who have no idea what that might entail) say, 'But it's Swiss-made!' So what? Do the Swiss (or the Japanese or the Swedes or Guatamalan Indians) have the edge on quality? The fact is, well-crafted items can come from anywhere — and so can sloppily built things.

Clutter by any other name is . . .

You can do a fairly good job of identifying junk by its nicknames — and they are legion. Cast a harsh eye on anything that you find yourself (or others) calling:

    doodas
    odds and ends
    curios
    knick·knacks
    paraphernalia
    collectibles
    bric-à-brac
    whatnots
    trifles
    trinkets
    baubles
    bits and pieces.

Chapter 12

You can take it with you ~ but don't!

Routine, too, can become junk.

Of course, we know we don't have to change geography to change routine, and that problems can travel with us to the farthest mountain cabin or desert island, but sometimes a change in location, leaving the usual routine and place behind, can force a freshess into your life that will make your heart beat with joy again and arouse new feelings (and revive some old ones).

Reflect on this one evening at the end of another day of routine. Maybe a trip to Africa or Australia or the Far East is out of the question, but if you curl up in your den of routine and security too long, your mate, family, peers, employers will see the same routine making you into a very dull person.

When our realm of experience is too confined, we lose confidence — get cluttered. (Isn't just about every unconfident person you know intensely territorial?) We don't give new people or places a chance to touch our hearts.

I'm not saying old friends or good old places are junk — just that we need to be always progressing and expanding. We can't stand still and savour a situation too long or it loses its savour. We have to go forward; we'll get junked standing still.

The same goes for the clutter of constantly returning to old stamping-grounds and scenes of former glory. Junk locks us into the old; it gives us false security. A return to jog memories or show the children or friends is sometimes beneficial, but make it quick and move on.

Things evolve, turn over — the new comes and the old dies or is left behind. Growth is all! Junk prevents growth, change, moving on ahead to better — in love, jobs, friendships.

There is always more ahead than behind; the past can become clutter to us if we don't learn to live it and leave it graciously behind.

You can take it with you... but please don't

We live in a mobile society; if we want to, we can move around pretty easily and

change our life experience. We can travel anywhere, any way, any day. We travel to and from work, to and from college, to and from relatives, to and from the places we go to just for the fun of it. We spend more time on the move than in our permanent living quarters, called home. The average person moves from one home to another about fourteen times during a lifetime.

Most of this mobility is for a few basic reasons:

1. To further our career.
2. To have new experiences.
3. To meet new people.

Much of our mobility is a quest for self-discovery and self-expression, but most of us don't really gain the advantage of our movement, or reach our real destination, because we're too weighed down by the clutter we take with us.

Most of us who want to get away from it all end up taking it all with us. The very things, the very people, the very thoughts that have ruined our nerves are packed (as much as possible) in the car or suitcase and taken with us. And then it has to be looked after, sorted and worried about as much in Majorca as back in the flat in Kensington or the house in Yorkshire.

We can't change, expand, meet new people, see new places or have new experiences when the old junk that inspired us to get away is travelling with us. Consider a simple trip into the country: we prepare for a three-day trip for five days — not what to do when we get there, but organizing getting there and back in comfort. We end up packing so much there's no room to sleep or sit. Excess baggage always dampens travel; much of it is clutter and ends up detracting from the pleasures of the place we're going to. Truthfully now — when you see someone staggering along with piles and piles of baggage, what do you think? You don't like them, do you?

Where you're going usually has a kitchen sink of some sort, so don't take yours along. The more junk you carry on your journey, the less holiday you'll have from junk.

When you're planning your next trip,

take a hard look at what you take and what you bring back: remember, the reason we move or go to places is often to get away from the things that make our lives cluttered and uncomfortable.

Here is a list of the things typical junkers lug on holiday and the bad reasons they give for taking them.

- **four outfits** for each projected day of the holiday — clothes for all different temperatures, weather and moods.
- the **dashing outfits** they never have the courage to wear at home (and won't have the courage to wear there)
- more **perfume** and **jewellery** than they ever wear at home
- **clothes** that are too tight for them at home (and will be even more impossible to wear after several days of feasting)
- at least two **formal outfits** in case they decide to go to a nightclub — but they'll never get off the beach, as usual
- **ten pairs of tights** (after the first sunburn, they won't be wearing any — though they *could* use them to hang themselves)
- **wide-brimmed hats** (hard to carry or pack without crushing them; hard to keep on, will block everyone's view if they do wear them and the car's rear window if they don't)
- **food** (in case they get stranded)
- a **can opener** (and an extra can opener)
- a **dressing gown** (and high-heeled mules)
- an **extra handbag**
- extra **heavy coat** and an extra raincoat
- all the **shoes** they never wear at home
- three **swimsuits** (different styles)
- **umbrella** and spare umbrella
- four boxes of **tissues**

- the **multi-vitamins** they never take at home
- six pairs of **sunglasses**
- a **sun lamp**
- **towels** they don't need
- **curling tongs** or electric curlers (they'll be too busy or too lazy to use either)
- a **cricket set**
- the **craft project** they never get round to at home (that somehow they're going to do amidst the exotic sights and sounds and happenings of wherever they're going)
- the last six months' **newspaper puzzles**
- the copy of *War and Peace* they promised their teacher they'd read.
- **unanswered letters** and outstanding personal accounting
- three **A4 pads** for the short story they're finally going to write.
- a **diary** with only three pages filled in (that will return with only three pages filled in)
- an **extra suitcase** (to lug home all those souvenirs)

And we wonder why we come home tired.

If you take it all with you, you might just as well not go. In fact, a better idea: once you have it all packed, just send all your junk on holiday — you'll both be better off.

A few tips for de-junking a suitcase.

1. Remember that just about everything can be replaced easily en route — except maybe spectacles and medicines.

2. The dry cleaner (or laundrette) where you're going can lighten your load on an extended stay. If you try to take enough for the whole trip, it'll just crush and crease anyway.

3. Don't bother to pack *food* — there's just about nowhere in the world you can go to and run out of food.

4. Don't stock up on films — you can buy films even at the most northerly tip of the Shetlands or at the foot of the Himàlàyas — every tourist stall has them. And are you sure you shouldn't just buy postcards? (Let *them* take the pictures.)

5. Pack it all up and try to carry it down the street — then start eliminating.

Don't forget the bags you carry every day

Make it a tradition, before you leave on any trip, to clean out your pockets, handbag and/or wallet. This will work wonders: (1) you'll leave clean and organized; (2) you'll be reminded of how much stuff you already have, and how much money you have to spend, just before you head off towards all those souvenir shops — it's a great junk inhibitor.

Souvenirs

In 1976 I took thirty-eight Boy Scouts on a trip.

At the spectacular Niagara Falls I observed only one boy once looking over into the awesome roaring tumble of water, absorbing the grandeur and the mist; the others — you guessed it — were stuck in a souvenir shop queue, shoving to latch on to gaudy mementos of the Falls.

But my Scouts were only small-time clutter collectors compared to us adults. We are souvenir-alcoholics; we feel we must buy. But almost everything we buy on holiday is junk — or ends up that way. We go to travel, to see new and different cultures, people, lands, places, scents, sounds, and to store the experience in our being — to replenish our souls, not our shelves.

We are often so obsessed with preserving memories with a souvenir that we're oblivious to the actual event or place we want to remember.

Souvenirs not only dilute the rapture of the moment, they cast their shadow over the entire trip. What is it, as you are flying or cruising, you suddenly worry about in one of your twelve suitcases? A £50 pair of shoes getting crushed, a £200 suit getting damp or creased? No — it's the £2.50 glass souvenir or the swan-shaped bottle of perfume that keeps you awake in your luxury suite at night.

Why do we load ourselves down with souvenirs? Maybe because we think people won't really believe we were there, so we feel we must return with evidence. But what will we do with the shell donkey from Polpero, the balsa canoe from Nigeria, the phial of sand from Alum Bay?

We buy all manner of often expensive souvenirs to prove to friends we were there. It would be cheaper and more legally convincing to carry a pocketful of affidavits and get them signed by the locals.

Not all silly souvenirs come off the shelves

Don't think because it didn't cost you money that it isn't a silly souvenir. What about that huge lump of driftwood you struggled home from Cornwall with, those pots of shells and bags of pebbles? Didn't they all leave their magic behind in the place where you found them?

Souvenirs cost

Oddly enough, when it comes to souvenirs, we lose all price perspective, even when we reach the till. We'll pay £5 for something worth 5p; I've watched people pay £15 for a cross-eyed bear that cost £1.50 to produce.

Even the best-controlled junker weakens when in another country — we'll travel a thousand miles to buy something that was generally available at home, pay twice as much for it and protect it on the trip better than our own health.

Would you go to a tourist trap in your own town and throw way £5 on a plastic model of your city hall? Of course not.

Don't buy junk under the guise of souvenirs! On your next trip try to bring home more memories and fewer memorabilia.

Litter louts

Some of us despoil the very places we go to admire by throwing our litter around. If you walked on the shore of a lake in Cumbria, during the holiday season, I bet you'd find plastic cups and bottles, lumps of polystyrene, drink cans, cigarette ends, broken glass, aerosol cans, even disposable nappies floating soggily at the edge of the water.

Animal litterers

Before all you animal lovers see what's coming and refuse to read on, let me bare my soul about animals. I've bred, fed, cared for and been around more animals, birds and fish than most people see in a lifetime and I love them. I think children need a pet as much as they need a good breakfast. The friendship of animals does a better job of restoring us to our senses than most things, but in some environments and situations, pets get turned into clutter and are cheated out of a decent life and the junk that results outweighs even the love we get from them.

Have you smelled a service layby, park or a street where people walk their dogs lately, or tried to get through one? It's like an obstacle course. I'll admit that inside the public loos where the humans do their thing isn't much better, but at least it's *contained*. The sanitation and health requirements for a house with two people living in it are an engineering nightmare of plumbing, piping and sewage systems. Yet in many places animals can clutter and litter and foul gardens and parks at will.

Carefree strolls through the park, lolling on the grass, playful tussles with your toddler are just a few of the joyous activities greatly inhibited by the mess left by dogs. No wonder there is a public uproar from time to time.

Chapter 13

Hooked on excess luxuries

No matter what we get, or where we go, our goal of 'having it made' always seems beyond our reach. That happiness, excitement, inexhaustible drive of youthful thinking and wanting and doing is gone—we don't have it. We want to get off, walk away from it all, maybe start again . . .

But someone or something has convinced us that we have to have a luxurious flat, bedsit or house with all the trimmings in order to be happy — and maybe two of them, one in a warm and one in a cool area of the world. A 'nice' home was once interpreted as a comfortable, pleasing, convenient dwelling. Now a nice home is 'Junk Plush', with hoarded or collected things propped up and hung up everywhere.

When and if all this is obtained, most people find that the effort of maintaining ownership offsets the benefits. If all of us honestly reflected back to the time in our lives of greatest satisfaction and enjoyment, when everything seemed to vibrate with feeling and freedom, it was

when life was simplest. Joy, energy and motivation come from relationships, discovery, creativity and accomplishment. Somewhere along the line all of these were squeezed out by piles (or structures) of junk.

Not satisfied with one house full of clutter, we dream of another, which in itself becomes clutter.

The second home

Ex-junkees can produce more impressive testimonies than active junkers, so I offer you a personal experience. During our final year at college my wife Barbara and I chose a beautiful sixty-acre place in southern Idaho, and in the next few years built a pleasant home in which to bring up our children. We had everything — creek, springs, trees, snow, hills, good neighbours, clean air, an unequalled view of the mountains — even mosquitoes! But during all that time we were thinking (as millions do), 'wouldn't a *second* home in the mountains be nice?' A good contract for my cleaning company made it necessary to move to Sun Valley for the summer. We left our sprawling new ranch house behind and stayed in Sun Valley for six years. We decided to build another house there and did so, drawing up the plans and doing all the work — plumbing, wiring, carpeting, etc. — ourselves. When it was time to return to the ranch, we decided to keep our Sun Valley house as a second home; we could afford the payments and had hundreds of friends who could use it for ski trips. We kept it for a year and ended up paying much more than the mortgage.

That house robbed me of more emotional energy than anything I've ever owned. Instead of thinking about how my son and the Cub Scouts were doing, how my daughter was getting on with her new job, how my wife might be feeling, I'd be thinking about the house — and wondering if the users had flushed the toilets, if the sprinkler had been drained, if the gate on the creek side was closed, if the beetles were boring the pines, if the last mountain storm had done any damage to the aerial. The house was out of sight, but ownership kept it from being out of mind. I felt compelled to rent it out and use it simply because I possessed it; all I seemed to have was unappreciative borrowers and people who didn't pay the rent. When I finally de-junked that house from my life, my goodness, it felt good!

Since then I've paid special attention to the topic of second homes. Almost everyone dreams of one, and almost everyone who has one spends every spare minute worrying about it, and every last penny repairing and paying for it. Only once in a while do they experience the pleasure of relaxing in it.

Millions of people who feel they're on the merry-go-round of life, the Excess Express, want to get off: they think they want to live in a little cottage in the country. What they're *really* saying is that they want to be de-junked of their dreary routine. If most of us de-junked our homes and lives, we could have that little dream cottage right where we live now — and it would cost us nothing.

The drive to have and to accumulate

Everyone wants more, better — and often faster. Someone once said that hell is full of people who were never satisfied.

Never being satisfied can be a virtue — if the longing, the lust, the living is for things that are meaningful to you personally and to those you love. Too many people judge worth almost entirely by accumulation. It takes a lot of whacks on the side of the head before we finally realize that many of the things we've accumulated, at great expenditure of time and effort, are and will only ever be clutter. Things are seldom permanent and unless used they are worthless. But accumulated good health, talent, friends, experiences and sensations are stored in us and are always there to reinvigorate and renew us all the years of our lives.

I heard a farmer who already owned 1,500 acres say, 'I don't want all the land in the world — just all that borders me.' That of course included all the land in the world, because it *all* bordered him. A certain maturity comes with accepting the fact that we can't have all the land, sex, food, money and power in the world. We probably have more of the 'all' than we can handle now, and anything beyond what we can use is junk. Sharing of self is the greatest satisfaction of all, and making better use of what we already have is the highest standard of living. Go for quality — not quantity!

Get it out of your head that you need a large selection to be happy. As a professional painter, I found that the more colour samples I showed to clients the more indecisive they became — and when they did choose between three shades that no one would ever be able to tell the difference between, they always whimpered, after it was on the wall, about which of the other two colours might have been better. One paint company recently brought out 1,322 new colours; I bet the psychiatry business boomed when they hit the market.

Clutter doesn't enrich life, it ends up confusing it. Happiness comes from loving and being loved: a giant selection of *things* just exhausts our spiritual, physical, and emotional energy. Sorting and decision-making can occupy our every waking minute.

'Things' always complicate matters. When the last rumble of the latest earthquake here in Idaho subsided, and the costs were counted, no lives were lost — but there was £500 million worth of damage. And it was labelled a 'natural disaster'. Had the same earthquake occurred in the same area one hundred years earlier, the cost of the damage might have approached £500 — and it would have been called a 'natural tremor'. Most of the destruction was to property — buildings — and their contents. No lives were lost because the worst-damaged buildings were unoccupied. The tremors only threatened a mass of *things*.

Increase is a confusing thing to deal with, because we must, to be happy, *increase* our wisdom, knowledge, friends, travel, experiences, opportunities, abilities, sense of self-worth and security. Increase is growth, and our possessions do sometimes have to increase with our growth — individuals, families, minds and businesses that do more usually need more tools, space and options. But somewhere the 'more' becomes extra and then a normal natural occurrence — like the earthquake — because of our junk, becomes a disaster instead of an experience.

Be careful with 'if I could only have . . . .'

Generally, by the time you can afford it you either don't want it, haven't the time or energy for it, or it means nothing to you.

I was brought up with enough of everything, but never any of the 'extra' or 'nice' things that other children seemed to have. Like you, I always thought that if I had more and better stuff I'd be happier and generally better off. When I went to the cinema every couple of months I was always captivated by the big glass sweet counter. It was ten feet long and two feet deep — and many times I pictured myself lying in there slurping and munching whatever I wanted. But I could only do some vicarious inner slurping and walk by.

For years I worried and wished, wished and worried about all those sweets. Then when I was eighteen, I worked in the evenings at a nearby cinema. I was completely in charge of that gleaming glass counter and was told to help myself to whatever I wanted. I went elbow-deep into those brimming containers, gorging myself on an array of formerly unattainable goodies — only to discover they were more exciting to look at and think about than to eat. I never again craved for sweets.

How many hours of life, mind and emotion we waste wanting and wishing

for things we don't need; ninety nine per cent of the time possessing it wouldn't make us happy.

Next time you're driving through the countryside or town, run this thought through the 'acquiring' section of your brain: If every person in the whole world disappeared and suddenly everything, I mean absolutely *everything,* was yours — fields, factories, bridges, buildings, ships, planes, vehicles — what would you do with them? What good would they do you? If you think it through, you'd realize you'd mainly have the problem of trying to work out how to use and care for all this.

One day I had the sudden realization: If I stopped buying things right away, there is no way I could ever use all I have *now.*

A friend of mine once thought up an idea to increase our awareness of what we possess, rich and poor, compared to 'poorer' countries of the world: he talked an ordinary family in India into moving every single thing they owned out onto the road in front of their house, after which he took a picture. It didn't take *them* long, but (the horrifying thought now crosses your mind) how would you or even *could* you do the same with all you own? It would take weeks; you'd need a wide-angle lens; you'd have to do it house by house in each neighbourhood, each on a different day, because there wouldn't be room in the road for both your and your neighbour's junk. And then would you actually have the guts to stand in front of it for a picture?

We are a society of surplus — most of us have more of everything than we need: food, money, possessions, time and attention. And after we've used what we need, we foolishly spend our time trying to use the surplus. I've watched people slave and scrounge and scrimp and hoard to earn more than they need — then spend the second half of their lives trying to protect the surplus from thieves and taxes. For some reason, when people finally get into a position of security and advantage, when they're finally in a position to have more choices, they inevitably — instead of choosing the avenues that would give them more ease and freedom to enjoy things — begin to fill up their homes and gardens with expensive porcelain dolls, extra TVs, prestigious books, overpriced paintings, complex gadgetry, complicated light fixtures, dozens of extra cooking and eating utensils, automatic barbecues and garden luxuries.

They take others out to dinner and show off their art collections, houses and cars because that's all they have to offer. What do you have to offer — a gem of thought? advice? example? encouragement? companionship? Or just some worthless *things?*

Junking the simple activity

We have so many things that they end up complicating and distracting our lives instead of enhancing them. It took us a while, and a lot of ingenuity, to find a way to clutter up even the simplest of pleasures. But now it's not at all uncommon for the preparation to require more skill than the sport or activity.

Fishing was once a quiet inexpensive way to relax and enjoy a challenge — until junk took over. The free bait worm was replaced by a £4.95 lure, the willow stick by an expensive graphite rod. The cost of catching a fish has soared from practically nothing (thinking about my last trip, with all the trimmings — flies, floats, lead weights, fish enticers, insect repellents, a water temperature gauge, etc., etc.) to about £75 per pound. It's not

only a project to decide on a place to go fishing and all the gear to do it with — it's hard to afford it, and it takes hours to get our equipment together (including a lot of junk that no self-respecting fish would bite).

We've taken a simple exercise like running and made it seem impossible to do without accessories. We begin, from the feet up, to deck our bodies out with special shoes, cushioned socks, knee supports, all sorts of stylish tracksuits, shorts, shirts, headbands, stereos, mileage meters (and would you believe it, the other day I got a catalogue selling a 'jogging stick' to help you keep your balance when you run, complete with a computer to tell you how far you've run and calculate how tired you are. It has a calendar and clock on it, too, just in case you get carried away in your jogging and lose track of what day it is!).

We don't need exercise equipment to exercise any more than we need a uniform to play any kind of ball game.

Once back-packing was a simple, get-away-from-it-all pursuit. People who delighted in setting off into the countryside taking only the bare essentials for survival, knew the art of travelling light yet being prepared for all nature might throw at them. However, manufacturers of camping gear have got in on the act and persuaded all would-be back-packers that now they can take all home comforts with them because these comforts have been miniaturized, made out of lighter than air materials, designed to fold away into a handy pack. The results are that trains of back-packers, looking more like pack ponies than carefree hikers, can be seen toiling through rugged countryside lugging with them fold-away stoves, blow-up mattresses, natty music centres, water

purifying tablets, insect repellent, inflatable canoes, and, for all I know, computerised compasses.

Consider, too, the pocket knife and the hunting knife. These two plain old knives won the West and carved the history of early America: skinned wild game, whittled whistles for the kids and, later, cut willow for wiener roasts. Now there are, conservatively estimated, 1,600 versions of speciality knives for the 800 jobs each of the other two plain old knives did (and still can do as well).

We've even managed to complicate telling the time. We worked on the old practical pocket watch for a century and finally got it so gilded and engraved and chained that it was too nice and too risky to carry so we have to leave it at home and ask our friends the time. (It was eventually used to start family quarrels over 'who gets Grandpa's watch'.) What a fate for a timepiece! It's nice to have diamonds, compasses, depth gauges and tiny gold ingots to greet you when glancing at the time, but it's certainly complicated.

Glasses to help us see better were so simple at first, we couldn't stand it. It didn't take long for the fitting and selection of the frame to take more time and money than the lenses. Once the main function of glasses was making us see better the things we were looking *at*. Now they've become so junked in style and design that our first consideration is how we look when others see us. It used to be easy to walk into an optician's and pick out a pair of frames — no more! Now you stand pop-eyed in front of glittering walls full of frames of every shape and colour, from the sleek gigolo look to the owly kind only squares used to wear. You're supposed to own glasses for every wardrobe change and mood — that is, when you're not wearing any of your three different kinds of contact lenses.

Crayons were the delight of all our childhoods — we had enough colour in eight little crayons to create anything we could imagine. When the 16-crayon box (double-decker) came out we were amazed — it even included grey! We didn't use all the colours, but the size of the packet made us and our parents feel good. Several years ago, though, I saw a sight that stunned me — a pack of thirty-two crayons; it had silver and gold and so many reds it shamed my teenage daughter's lipstick collection. But today I saw a giant box of sixty-four crayons, as big as a lunchbox and full of obscure exotic colours. A child could get an attack of nerves just picking the right shade.

Toys today are so junked they hardly need kids; today's toys can practically play by themselves. Consider the doll. Dolls have thrilled children for thousands of years. My four daughters, even when their dolls lost their hair, an arm, and the paint off their rubber lips, only loved them more. Then the doll designers appeared: closing eyes were great, a crying doll was greater; even *I* was impressed with the refreshingly different drinking and wetting models. Then realism began to crowd out imagination; we had walking models and talking models, dolls whose hair could be cut and curled.

Now you don't only need a doll: you need a doll cosmetic kit, a complete doll wardrobe for all four seasons (including holiday wear), a sports car, a beach buggy, an estate car, a bedsit, a TV and stereo system, a digital watch, legwarmers, tights, a pony, a poodle and a male companion for your doll. I expect to see mini cosmetic surgery gear in the next doll kit. But if you give a child a choice, do you think it'll pick that glamourous robot with the 38-inch bustline? Raggedy Ann will win every time!

Children don't get much satisfaction out of elaborate toys, because there's really not a lot a child can do with them — the *toys* do everything themselves. My wife and I learned this the Christmas our six children were aged two to eight. We shopped carefully and bought a mixture of games, a few puzzles, some educational toys, a couple of somersaulting monkeys, etc. That Christmas afternoon the children were halfheartedly pawing and pondering their treasures when a friend called with a sack of wood off-cuts for our fire — blocks sawed off 2x4s and 2x6s from a new house. He put the sack full of plain, crisp-smelling wood on the floor in front of the fireplace and the children descended on it and began constructing castles, fences, forts, houses and bridges. For days those ordinary pieces of wood held sway over all the brightly coloured, cleverly designed toys.

This experience taught us that children are most stimulated by all-purpose toys that their imaginations can run free with. A Planetfighter Orbitmaster 1234X with whirring engines and battery-operated lasers can't be anything but a Planetfighter Orbitmaster 1234X, and when the child is tired of outer space he ignores the toy.

Is more better?

Our ranch has a log house dating from 1880. It measures thirty-six feet by fifteen and has two rooms and an attic. Once, driving past it on the way to a concert, affluent acquaintances of ours observed how dreadful it must have been in the old days to live there. I reminded them that eleven children were brought up there, with no video games, no TV, no electricity, no fridge, no insect spray, no thermostats, only one clothes cupboard, an outside lavatory and spring water — and they were and have ended up to be a glistening, vibrant healthy tribe that lived long and happy lives with frequent smiles on their faces. The couple shook their heads in amazement, not comprehending how anyone could exist without the clutter comforts of life. I'm not advocating log-cabin living or camping in the local park, only pointing out that most social and psychological problems, those unpleasant ugly things that suck life and love out of us — like selfishness, despair, anxiety, intolerance, bigotry, financial failure, divorce, embezzlement, theft, murder, suicide, even war — result directly from our honouring of junk, our quest for ever more and ever more elaborate possessions.

Some people will laugh and say, 'Simplicity is fine for a change, but I love my comforts.' Next time you hear that, take a hard look at the person who says it, and you'll chart troubled waters. People who have a luxurious life say it's reassuring, that they feel confident surrounded by huge piles of things, even if they don't use them. But are those people really happy — with their lives and minds, buried in menu-reading, weight loss, fashion watching, colour-matching, land-owing, tax deductions, security checks, and the squabbles of children fighting over their piles of possessions.

I once met a beautiful elderly woman who radiated enthusiasm as she recalled living simply: 'We had a lovely, fully equipped home in the city that included velvet curtains and sets of silver and fine dishes. We had earned that place by working hard on a farm in the mountains. The 5,000-acre farm had no irrigation (only rainfall) and to operate it we had to move to the old ranch house there and live during the growing season. That house was the opposite of our nice town house. Here we kept only basic supplies, and my husband and I each had one tin plate and one tin cup, a knife, fork and spoon and

that was it — no extras, no luxury.' She glowed just thinking about it. 'In fact, my fondest memory of my youth and early married life is that old tin cup and plate. Food always tasted good on it, we didn't worry about it breaking or getting stolen, things were so simple, I could enjoy my family, our workers, the air, the leaves. For thirty years the memory of that tin cup has been a source of joy'.

She was feeling the rapture of dejunked living.

When the tin cup story is told, I notice everyone in the audience has a longing look. A tin cup isn't necessary for all of us, but the spirit of simplicity is, and will leave a better taste in our lives than crystal goblets.

On the ranch where I was brought up, because the main house was too small for all our family, my teenage brothers and I slept in a small unheated outhouse (I remember the brush cleaner in a glass jar freezing one night). To keep warm at night we'd heat up a little flannel bag of wheat and throw it to the bottom of the bed to take the chill off *and* we had outside toilets with all the trimmings.

Since then, I've stayed in the finest hotels, slept in the finest beds and eaten the finest food in the finest places in the world, but none has ever come close to the feeling of simple freedom of that outhouse. A de luxe sauna bath has never felt any better than the tin bath and kettle of hot water (even when I was the third one to bath in the same water). Again, I'm not recommending a return to primitivism, only reminding you that the things you feel and enjoy the most are the simplest and most basic. Because ownership of them allows you the time to enjoy them — you don't have to spend all your time paying for and maintaining them. It isn't the tin cup and plate that

you remember so fondly; it's the fact there weren't cabinets of china to look after and show off, velvet-lined boxes filled with silverware to insure, polish, store and worry about. 'We have sufficient for our needs' is a sentence of freedom from the old enemy, *clutter.*

Simplicity doesn't mean hard times; luxury doesn't mean good times. But we too often think of more as better, convenience as comfort — and that isn't so. It doesn't take a padded toilet seat or an electric blanket to mould good character, accomplishment, and feelings of aliveness and personal worth.

You can survive on a lizard diet

The joy of knowing you don't need junk to survive will be a dynamic motivator to you. When we read those survival stories about people making it through sub-zero weather with multiple injuries and without food, most of us sigh and think to ourselves, 'They must have had incredible nerve and endurance, a super will and sense of determination.' Not really. Those people are no tougher than you or me — they simply found out the strength of a human without junk! Allow me to relate another anecdote.

I met an energetic, self-assured woman who told me she once felt like a real loser. She was a little overweight and had a poor self-image as she dragged herself around her home, job and school. She had bought everything supposedly needed for a happy life — the best clothes, cars, furniture, holidays, season tickets, the whole gamut of goodies that spell 'success'. She'd even taken most of the courses that try to help you pull your life together to be happy and productive. Looking at her now, I couldn't picture her

no water, no nothing. He then turned us loose in the desert for a week, and we lived! Using nature — the ground, the air, the plants and all the other things that were just there — to do it. Instead of an unendurable hardship as I had dreaded, it. became an exhilarating experience. Self-confidence and self-assurance flowed into me with every drink out of a water cache or bite of a ground squirrel. I used to faint when I saw a mouse; now I was savouring lizard legs. Everything smelled and tasted and felt good because it was just me and what was there. When I finished the desert trip and course I knew for the first time in my life that I didn't need all those *things* I owned to be somebody. For the first time ever I really looked at and experienced the things around me — sunrise, sunset, a cactus flower, the wail of a coyote, the shape of a stone.

'I enjoyed peaceful sleep (even on hard ground!) My hair looked and felt better than it ever had before — without a hair drier or an array of shampoo and sprays and setting lotions and rinses. I felt fit and strong and alert all the time. That course did me the greatest favour of my life. It taught me that *I* determined my happiness and generated my own worth and enthusiasm for life — not all the trinkets, motivational cassette tapes or exotic getaway places. I learned to use what I *was* instead of what I *had*.'

That course did only one thing for this woman — it de-junked her. We don't all need to eat lizard stew in the desert — we can enjoy simple meals at home — but maybe if necessary some forcing of the issue might enlighten your life like it did hers.

as the lost soul she assured me she once was.

What happened? Well, it started with a summer course on wilderness survival at a local university. The teacher, a keenly experienced outward bound type named Larry Dean Olsen, had written a best-selling book, *Outdoor Survival Skills,* and offered a class on the same subject. I'll pass the woman's experience on to you in her own words: 'I enrolled in this class and Olsen told us we didn't need much to survive and live, that as humans we have amazing depth and adaptability. I hadn't tried starvation yet, so I decided to stick it out. After some preliminary instruction, he took us out to the edge of the desert, dressed in the simplest of clothes, armed with nothing but a little knife — no food,

Chapter 14

Destroying your body with junk

At the age of fifteen, for my Future Farmers of America agriculture project, I bought (with a little help from my dad) some baby bull calves. Their horns, at that point, were about three harmless inches long. One day dad brought home a box of all sizes of steel doughnut-looking weights. He explained to me that the horns of a bull of this breed, if left unattended, will grow straight out and up and long and be exceedingly dangerous, causing possible injury to fellow bulls — which even then were worth up to £500 when grown. But if weights were fastened on the ends of the horns, the horns would grow downwards in a beautiful curve, eventually making the animal both safe and attractive.

As that year progressed, we put larger and larger weights on the horns, and as the bulls grew the weight build-up was so gradual they didn't seem to notice and went merrily along. The interesting thing, however, was when the horns were finally curved correctly and the weights removed. As soon as we turned the bulls out of the chute with the big weights gone,

they walked slowly a few steps, shaking and twisting their heads, trying to work out what was different. They swung round, threw their heads up and down, first slowly, then rapidly, and suddenly discovered they had shed a heavy burden. In noble triumph, they arched their heads and tails in the air and thundered off in a happy cloud of dust and glory, feeling a new freedom from a bondage they had never realized they were suffering.

There isn't one of us who hasn't dreamed of rumbling off in a great cloud of glory, yet in reality, most of us have a hard time dragging, wheezing, waddling, creaking, coughing along, rising in the morning and getting through each day.

Well, you've already guessed why — it's the same reason we have trouble going through our drawers, our cupboards, our garages, etc. Clobber — we eat it, drink it, breathe it. A little here and a little more there, and like the weights on the bull, we gradually build up a burden we don't even realize we're carrying.

Stand in front of a mirror in a swimsuit or in the altogether and face it — many of

109

us are living, walking piles of clutter. Our bodies are like an old junk car; the outside (if patched and primed and repainted) might look good, like those who wear padded or compressing underwear and layers of cosmetics. But we're running rough, out of tune, out of stride and gradually putting ourselves out of circulation.

Like our other junk, we can't hide it. It

shows on us like a scowl. Who wants or likes a countenance clouded with clutter? A junk body is exactly like other junk — it blocks us off from the things that generate love and good feelings.

A cluttered physical condition robs a person of poise, dignity, motivation, self-respect, the joy of work and, believe it or not, even affects the mind and the spirit. Inspiration, enthusiasm and endurance cannot exist in a body or mind struggling to combat the influence of consumable clutter. If we're going to get out of the rut and gain confidence, beauty, affection, exhilaration, we have to de-junk the things that can take it from us.

If there is one thing in life we get tired of,

it's people preaching and advising and scaring us about what we eat, drink and breathe. Even before we were old enough to fully understand it, parents and other adults were shaking a warning finger at us and telling us what to eat and what not to eat and even how much and when. As we were growing up, our health teacher, the games teacher, the media and a famous doctor in every issue of *Reader's Digest* were still outlining the perfect diet of life. New fads and health foods and drinks spun by us like meteors, until I really think we became immune to it all. Some great scientist is always warning us of guaranteed early death or disease from some eating, drinking or breathing violation. We glance at it and say to ourselves, 'Ah well, I've heard that before.' Ten years ago cranberries were causing cancer, now they're supposed to prevent it; they tell us that we should avoid cholesterol, then that it isn't really necessary. Who can we trust? And so we shrug it off, maybe filing a little of it away in our minds. And now when we're reading Aslett's book on clutter in sneaks that message again on food and drink and breathing. Why don't you forget all the advice and warnings, and for the rest of this chapter just rely on yourself — who you are and how you feel, and how you *want* to feel. It's surprising just how much you know about yourself and your own health and feelings. For once listen to yourself instead of the coaching, promising and prophesying of any outsider — even me.

First, remember your thoughts at the time of sickness (yours or others') or death; the times when you're down and feeling heavy, tired, unresponsive; the times you've said to yourself, 'How vain and useless all my efforts and plans and ownership are, how completely my values are thwarted and attainments wiped out if I have no get-up-and-go.' Position, money, opportunity, possessions, even loved ones have limited value if we aren't feeling vibrantly well and full of energy.

When it comes to the things we consume, we seem to have a built-in sense of what is good for us and bad for us. We don't always listen to ourselves, but we do know. Listen for the next days —and before, during and after consumable clutter is taken into your life, you'll hear:

'I know this is a bad habit but. . . .'
'I've really got to cut down on this, or stop.'
'This is definitely not good for me but. . . .'
'Good thing there are indigestion pills, pass some more of the. . . .'
'This dessert is divine . . . I'm wicked to eat it, but. . . .'
'I've got to kick this habit. . . .'
'One of these days this is going to do me in. . . .'
'Oh, I really shouldn't . . . you know what it does to me. . . .'

You'll hear a hundred variations of this, but they're all the same. We basically know what is good for us, what we should and shouldn't consume, because we know how we feel after partaking of it.

Doctors and dietitians preach de-junking our life so we'll live longer. A greater quantity of life *is* a benefit, but a better *quality* of life is our ultimate reason for de-junking.

We should de-junk our diet, not only to live longer, but so we can live and feel better *now*. So what if we do live longer — if we're miserable and ill-tempered all the time, what good is longer life to us?

Every one of us could sit down right now and make a list of things we're consuming that are junking and clogging up the circuits of our lives. We already know what they are, we just haven't started dealing with them.

Eating your heart out?

I learned an interesting fact about junk food from a park ranger's lecture: 'Junk food has weakened the big healthy Yellowstone bears. The bears' natural diet of wild fruits and berries, insects and fish left them with a thick layer of quality fat to carry them through hibernation. But begging beside the road from junk food toting tourists, eating potato crisps, sweets, biscuits, white bread, spreads, etc., out of refuse bins doesn't nourish the bears — hence some don't make it through the winter.' Besides giving those noble bears sleepless nights, junk food is:

- **Overpriced . . .**
- **Overseasoned . . .**
- **Oversweetened . . .**
- **Overpreserved . . .**
- **Overpackaged . . .**

It affects us adversely in several ways.

Physically
We don't have any stamina when we feed ourselves with junk food. Junk food is full of empty calories — high in fat, sugar, salt and 'fillers' that yield little real nutrition. It raises our blood pressure, sends our blood sugar skyrocketing, then crashing, clogs and hardens our arteries, and promotes tooth decay.

Emotionally
Junk food either depresses or overstimulates us.

Aesthetically
Isn't is ugly to see people gorge, slurp and stuff rubbish food? And to see what becomes of their bodies afterwards?

Financially
Junk food often costs a lot (considering what it's manufactured from and what

results it yields)-but it returns little. And it costs a fortune to manufacture and dispose of the packaging.

Spiritually
Junk food encourages undisciplined indulgence.

Full-course clutter

Junk food damage isn't confined to making people fat, immobile and polluted; consumption and desumption have become a time-consuming ceremony instead of a necessity to get on with life. There is barely a place we can go where food is not the featured focus — the main event. Conferences, gatherings, meetings, parties, services, cinemas, parks — all flash food in our faces constantly. We can't come up with any genius when our mind is constantly cluttered and interrupted by dining, sipping, slurping, guzzling, sloshing, chomping, puffing, etc. Junkers are always munching or shoving something in their faces — and trying to shove it in ours.

We spend three or four hours a day in expensive elaborate eating rituals and then have to spend an hour or two (and more money) at the health clinic or tennis court swishing at tennis balls or lurching around the track trying to work it off — what a waste of life. If you waste just thirty extra minutes a day at meal times, that's enough time in one year to write a dozen magazine articles or go on fifteen fishing trips — 182 hours you could have spent with your children or friends or spouse.

Thirty ways of ruining a potato

Food in its natural state is full of vitamins, minerals, protein, fibre and

flavour. Processing and overcooking strip food of nutrients and taste; we then overcompensate for its lack of natural taste with sauces, additives and salt, salt, salt. We can junk perfectly good food beyond recognition.

We go to lavish seafood restaurants to savour the delights of the ocean, order a dish of 'Crab à la Expensive', then dip that good crab in gunky seafood sauce until it's not only coated but saturated, which leaves the crabmeat totally untasteable. We could just as well have dipped a piece of bread in the sauce and eaten it, for all the difference it makes.

Being a potato grower, I can't believe how a nice spud (high in protein, iron and vitamin C) can be transformed into a fried strip of grease or a soggy shell of toppings and fillings. (My next book will probably be *Thirty Ways to Ruin a Good Idaho Potato*.) In its original splendour it's so good and so

112

simple; junked up, 'prepared', or 'processed' it's unrecognizable and unhealthy.

Purity and simplicity are everyone's favourite haven. We travel to remote northern mountains to breathe pure air and fragrant pine, to sip from fresh streams. We enjoy everything in its pure and simple state but we seem to forget this the minute something is put before us on a platter. On a trip to Alaska once, our guide hauled in some crystal-clear glacier ice, thousands of years old; it looked like a handful of diamonds. As he passed it round for the group to taste, one woman asked eagerly, 'Can we put some chocolate syrup on it?' Without realizing it, we've come to thinking that any edible thing in its natural state is plain or 'bland'. This is not so.

We're forever fussing with our food — putting ketchup on it, syrup on it, barbecue sauce on it. I'm not saying we should throw all our condiments and dressings away, but we ought to question why we use so many. Is it just habit? Does food really taste so awful without glop on it? If so, it's probably overcooked or overprocessed — or both.

Those who indulge ... bulge!

Even good food, like good merchandise, is clutter if we don't need it, don't have a place for it, or can't afford the consequences of it.

Look around the next time you travel, at school, at parties, at supermarkets, at amusement parks, in travel terminals, at the beach or in the street — people are strained-looking, puffy, bloated from junk.

Bow-fronted sights abound on every side — thirty-year-old men with bulging bellies; chubby little junior school kids with chocolate dripping from their lips; overweight women who can no longer walk and now waddle.

It's pathetic to see a woman in gross physical condition spend £50 on a hair and nail job. Her junk fat will be the first thing noticed, completely undoing the superb coiffure and manicure. It's equally sad to see a puffy-cheeked young man, belly lapping over a perfectly tailored new suit, trying to look impressive.

If we're carrying extra pounds, it's clutter. It will not only weigh us down every step of the way but very few people have real tolerance for, or faith in, fat people. Alas, poor physical condition speaks for itself, and none of us likes what it says about us or others. Making up your mind to de-junk is the best diet plan going...

Saviour of the morsel

So many of us seem to have the consuming urge to devour every ounce and crumb ever placed in front of us. A classic example of this is when we're on a plane or at a party — we're already so full of food we'd like to lie down, but when the hors d'oeuvres tray or the service trolley comes along, we feel we must get our money's worth. The thought of those salted peanuts and sugary beverages and fatty ham bits just lying there and going to waste haunts us to the very centre of our junk gland. It we don't save them, they'll go to waste.

Ridiculous, isn't it, that we feel this inner calling to be 'Saviour of the Morsel'.

People are fed twice on the flight between London and New York — it would be more efficient to install self-feeders in the armrests. If the flight were delayed and the stewardesses kept

113

serving, the passengers would bloat themselves out of existence. We are quick to ridicule the pig — an intelligent animal that never makes a hog of himself!

De-junking's most dignified words - 'no thanks'

Just because much of the junk we're offered is 'free' doesn't mean we're obliged to take it. No matter what Mother used to say, we are *not* in duty bound to eat everything set in front of us. Just because the creamed potatoes or the french fries or the Yorkshire pudding 'comes with it' — it's not divine edict that we eat until we're uncomfortable. Thousands of restaurants are serving and wasting food whether we eat it or not. And we're even *less* obliged to eat beyond capacity at someone's home, where the food is unlikely to be wasted.

I don't know whether it's instinct to eat food all up, but we'll go to foolish extremes to avoid wasting it. There we were, a vanful of tourists almost upon the Canadian border when my wife announced, 'Oh, good grief! Our sack of apples. They're going to take it away from us at the customs.' The only way to protect our investment seemed to be to consume the apples. We had just eaten — no one needed or wanted to look at a Cox's Orange Pippin — but we grimly worked out how many each of us had to eat and stuffed ourselves until we felt sick. The thought of surrendering to loss often overcomes our good sense. The apples had very little value and were certainly clutter under those circumstances. Leaving them at the border wouldn't have hurt, but isn't it hard to give up something! (By the way, they *didn't* take them and we were miserable the rest of that day.)

The compulsion to 'save it' or 'get my share' is responsible for a lot of extra pounds and inches. Enough is never enough.

Let's have a hot cup of ... clutter?

Let's take a look at one of the most popular drinks going, good old coffee. Some people really enjoy their coffee and probably will continue to forever, but what do most coffee drinkers, of the thousands we know, have to say in their own words about the habit? 'I really need to cut down on my coffee or stop altogether.'

Apart from not helping nerves or heart or kidneys or stomach, what does the coffee habit really do for us? It takes hours of time out of our lives. We can't work at home or at the office without the inevitable wait for coffee. Often the whole operation has to be held up or delayed to get (or clean up after) coffee. Coffee often comes before calls, children or appointments — shouldn't it worry us that we can't seem to function without it?

It's distracting to meet with or do business with someone who has to sip, stir, gulp and gurgle coffee down all through the conversation.

Coffee spillage clean-up in my country (in clothes, furniture, carpets, buildings, vehicles, even planes) is a multi-million-pound job. And with the coffee habit comes all manner of pots, grinders, cups, mugs, filters, strainers and tools to administer it (and clutter our lives).

It's the time they take out of our lives that ultimately makes many habits questionable. Watch some of the more efficient people you know working. You'll notice that they aren't necessarily any better or more skilled or faster workers than you — they just don't have themselves burdened with so many junk things and so much personal consumption clutter.

Try to work out exactly what the allure of coffee is for you. Half the time when you rush to the coffee machines for a 'fix' you notice, an hour later, that you never did take more than a sip or two of it. Do you *really* like the taste of coffee? Are you sure a hot cup of anything wouldn't fill the 'ritual' role just as well?

Junk on the rocks

Taking a long look at results, can you think of even *one* positive effect that outweighs the harm alcohol does to life and society? (Yes, the industry employs people, but so does disease, war, fires, etc.) The manpower, fixtures, hardware, and utensils it takes to make alcohol available at social events are often more trouble than the food. Yet thousands of deaths a year in the U.K. are related directly to alcohol, and the cost of alcohol abuse is a burden on millions of individual taxpayers, families and businesses, as well as on the government.

Just like junk food and soft drinks, alcohol is full of empty calories. It robs your body of vitamins. Alcohol is a *drug,* remember, and drugs should be used carefully, not carelessly. Alcohol is also a toxin — you can kill yourself with a single bottle of whisky if you can pour it down you fast enough and manage not to throw up. Why do you think hangovers feel so bad? Your body has been poisoned!

Remember, too, how silly (or disgusting) people who've had too many drinks look and sound: wobbling in their seats (and on the way to the loo), talking too loudly (and loosely), spilling things, slurring their speech — do you really want to be like that?

No matter what anybody tries to tell you, you don't *have* to drink to be macho, chic, sociable or even polite. There might be magic in moderation, but remember, 'one or two' is only too likely to start a collection.

Carbonated clutter

Much of this logic applies also to the excessive use of soft drinks and colas. Of the junk habits I gave up, this is the one I miss least. It was a relief to be able to eat and travel and visit people without one of those bubbling drinks forever in front of me.

Do you have a soft drink constantly clutched in your hand? Colas, and other sodas too, inject caffeine, sugar and all manner of chemical sweeteners, flavourings and colourings into our systems, harming healthy bodies and appetites. I really shudder, though, when I see children running around with bottles of pop. The sugar rots their teeth and the chemicals make them hyperactive. Milk, juice or water would be more nutritious — and cheaper.

The soft drink habit is a nuisance to handle and maintain. Pop cans, bottles and containers, full and empty, are all over the place, filling the food cupboard, refrigerator, freezer and lorry. We get so used to it we think it's an essential part of our life. But like other clutter, it can be disposed of easily, benefiting us immensely.

We get tired of other people harping on what's good and not good for us, but we swallow the advertising that tells us. They even tell us what tastes good and we swallow *that.* I think of this every time 'helpful hint' books tell me how great cola is to clean the toilet. As a cleaning expert I have to nod affirmatively — it *does* work. The simple reason (read the can/bottle) is that it contains phosphoric acid. Phosphoric acid is what we professional cleaners use to help dissolve lime, mineral and hard-water build-up in bathrooms. I have a friend who even uses cola to clean road film off his camper. For some reason I can generate no enthusiasm for drinking a good lavatory bowl cleaner.

Mental and physical addiction to fizzy lemonade is pathetic — it's just one more cup of calories and carcinogens. The most refreshing thing you can do is de-junk.

Junk food generates junk

The next time you're walking down a street, notice that you're walking amidst litter and clutter and rubbish on every side. Notice that most of it is wrappers from junk food, cans and bottles from junk drinks, butts of cigars and cigarettes, chewing gum from gum chewers. As you look at it, think. As a professional cleaner/restorer/repairer/replacer, I can say from experience that junk habits cause some of the greatest maintenance expenses. And smoking is the most expensive consumable clutter of all.

Incendiary clutter

Seeing that we all (even the smokers among us) agree that smoking is a junk habit, let's look at how it leads to numerous undesirable results.

1. **It hurts you**
   Not only is this habit likely to make you die sooner and more painfully, but it will cloud and retard your social life. Fondling, fumbling with, carrying, caring for and storing smoking materials steals valuable

time and tarnishes your image (yes, even you sophisticated pipe smokers — smoking projects a negative image.) Smoking can cut you off from opportunities, jobs, relationships. Who enjoys interacting with a person who constantly clutches and nurses a cigarette? It has a negative effect on your appearance, as well as your health. It labels you as unconfident, uncaring — and mates, friends and bosses will treat you accordingly. Who really wants to see smoking secretaries, receptionists, doctors, cooks, teachers, cab drivers, caretakers, companions? Smokers are often avoided or passed over because of their junk habit. (And nobody *really* wants to kiss a smoker.)

2. **It hurts others**
   Smoking is unquestionably inconsiderate. Eyes water, lungs fill with smoke, clothes and hair are saturated offensively. Who would consider taking out a miniature incinerator and burning paper, leaves and refuse whenever they got the urge? That's what a smoker does.

   Second-hand smoke, as a rule, is worse than the filtered original — and the smoker doesn't give the victim a choice. Most non-smokers find smoke unpleasant, but for people with respiratory problems — asthma, bronchitis, hay fever — contact with cigarette smoke can be downright dangerous. Many people sensitive to smoke have to avoid restaurants, pubs and theatre foyers because the atmosphere there is about as poisonous as the surface of Venus.

   Lighting up a cigarette in someone's home, car or · presence without asking permission is the height of immaturity. It's plain rude to force ugly, smelly junk on others. And friends and family have to service this junk habit: they have to clean up after you, provide you with an area, receptacles etc., to accommodate your junk habit, and they hate it.

Last but not least, smoking sets an awful example to youth. What kind of parents or grandparents would be uncaring enough to inflict such a junk habit on their offspring?

3. **It damages property**

All of us pay a small fortune for the smoking habit — it costs taxpayers thousands of pounds daily. An alarming amount of clutter, litter and building damage, indoors and out, is caused by smoke.

Smoking also causes a high percentage of fatal and damaging fires' and makes conditions on many jobs unsafe.

As a professional maintenance and cleaning consultant, I'm appalled when I see a person stand on a new floor or carpet, or sit in a nice upholstered seat, and crush and throw away one cigarette after another, or fill an ashtray with stubbs. The smoke is dirtying the windows, yellowing the light fixtures above, cutting the efficiency of energy expenditure, soiling and ruining the polystyrene ceiling tiles, impregnating the upholstery, and burning and damaging the carpet and floor. A smoker does as much (or more) physical damage to the building as the person who throws a chair through the window — yet it's the window-breaker we'd haul off to prison. Many millions of pounds could go to

wages — or profits — instead of cleaning and repairing the damage caused by smokers. In trying to correct the problem, we designate special smoking areas, make better filters, bigger ashtrays, better vents and room deodorizers, better gargles and toothpastes, develop lung transplants, etc., but this is like building a bigger drawer, cupboard or garage when the others get full; the clutter is still there, doing damage, only contained.

The simplest, cheapest, most effective and rewarding approach is to de-junk the habit; then the problem will be cut off at the source. This is the beauty of de-junking. Instead of hacking at the strangling mass of leaves and branches, we cut the root — de-junk!

On not being a dope

If you take unnecessary drugs, you may be too far gone to de-junk. Pills and powders aren't the answer — look deep into your heart — find out the cause of your anxiety. De-junk *that* from your life and you'll be able to throw out most drugs, too. It's a very simple fact — though sometimes difficult to accept — that the use of any substance that enslaves us robs us of our freedom of choice. Like all junk, it ends up making the choices for us. Shakespeare summed it up pretty well:

'Oh God, that men should put an enemy in their mouths to steal away their brains.' If you live sensibly (without junk) and know how to deal with stress (de-junking helps here, too), you shouldn't need pep pills, tranquilizers, muscle relaxants or stimulants. Many physical ailments you're taking medication for might disappear with de-junking, too.

Chapter 15

People can be junk?

When you have finished throwing clutter out of your drawers, shelves, car, workshop, purse, tummy, etc., you'll feel *almost* pure and free; your life will *almost* breathe new meaning. I say 'almost' because there's still something bothering you, some junk hovering around somewhere, about to pop into your life and reclutter it. What is it? You can't see a thing hanging on or around you; you've followed this book to the letter. Nothing could be left; why, you're so pure of junk you feel disinfected! You can't work out what that growing anticipatory ache is... Until *rinnnnnnng* – it's the phone or it could be the door. Suddenly you realize that secret irritation is not some*thing* — but some*body*.

Truthfully now, aren't there a few people in your life you just hate to see coming? They might be nice people, too, but when they appear (in person or voice), a shudder or sigh of boredom escapes you, and you only relax when you see their car lights go out of sight or hear the final click of the phone.

There are people who, no matter how hard they try to be friends, clutter your whole being — cause discomfort and conflict in you. They're generally the type who begin a conversation with 'Guess who this is' or 'Are you doing anything?' and usually end it with, 'Well ... er ... could I have/could you spare ...' Every day they waste forty-five minutes of your life with phone calls detailing their gizzard operation, their bowel trouble, their petrol mileage, their children's exam results. Their only objective is to use up time or make you aware of their problems (which you could do without). Do you like your life being interrupted, questioned, analysed, scheduled, infringed upon by someone — anyone — just whenever he or she feels like it?

No matter how good their intentions, no matter how distinguished their accomplishments, no matter how hard we try not to come to this conclusion, some people's presence can junk up our lives worse than a refuse lorry unloading on our lawn.

The little boy who wore the T-shirt that said, 'I ain't junk, 'cause God don't make no junk' was right, but man makes junk and plenty of it, and not all of that junk is just the *things* around him. People let themselves get worthless; they do worthless things, have worthless conversations, spend time in worthless pursuits, learn worthless precepts and — although they look and breathe like normal people, are rich or poor, have a high position or low — they can become junk because in general they are useless almost to anyone, including you.

Could it be that a friend, a longstanding associate, a companion, a fellow worker or board member, an employee, a customer, or even a partner could be clutter? It could be so.

Any of these sound familiar?

A team mate: at first you thought it was his bad breath, his squeaky shoes and his loud laugh that bothered you, but every night of league play the glory of the sport is dampened because old loud-laugh is going to be there. He can't keep his hands off you, he can't keep his conversation out of your business and personal life, he never chips in on the petrol money. He's like a cancer, growing stronger — it's time to de-junk.

You went to high school with her and were chums, you both twittered and giggled and messed around. You parted ten years ago; she kept on twittering, you grew up and got some class. You end up in the same town; she comes over every day and wants to hang around and rehash long-gone school gossip, the history of who married who, her new shade of nail polish, her unimaginative holidays, her sexual frustrations — all the while ignoring her four children playing

Tarzan on your curtains. You are either going to lose her as a friend or lose several years of your life: it's time to de-junk.

You've been lovers for longer than you can remember. He's clever, funny, charming. He also drinks too hard and works too hard and his flat is filthy. You worry about his drinking, his bad stomach, his insomnia; he tells you you nag. You try to help him as much as you can without fussing; but you suddenly realize that he's self-destructive and he's taking you with him. Your self-esteem is at rock bottom; you're not doing him any good and it's slowly killing you. Great vibes or no, you'd better de-junk him, you'll save yourself and the shock may make him get the help he needs.

We've all met the 'promoter', the high-flying wise-guy who's always letting you in on the secret of a get-rich-quick deal that hasn't made *him* rich yet, but will you. He spends all his time scheming, conning to make the 'big profit'. He always finds or has fantastic profit deals going, sure-fire schemes that will return great amounts of money, instant power and fame. He completely ignores all his previous failures with remarks like: 'Well, that fell through because of the change in the economy, but this new deal. . . .' He bleeds his friends and relatives, the old and the young, yet never seems to have anything himself except great enthusiasm to put together another 'great and promising' deal. Do yourself a favour and do some de-junking.

You come home and see that certain car there, and your stomach tightens and sinks. 'Come on,' you reason with yourself, 'they're my relatives, God-fearing, respectable — but oh heavens, I

thought we'd moved far enough away...'
You need to de-junk because that sick
feeling won't leave until they do.

You've been an employer for ten years,
you've aided, counselled, paid,
instructed, insured, etc., a person who
seems to steadily be getting more removed
from the reality of his job and causing you
and fellow employees constant irritation.
Soon you spend all your time trying to
avoid contact, you are of no mutual
benefit — it's all agony He's doing little
but taking your emotional energy, not
just your financial resources. If he can't or
won't change, it's time to de-junk.

Remember that sometimes you can
take a reverse approach with a junker
who's cluttering up your life. If you're
locked in a job, place, school or
association with a person or persons who
make your life steadily more unbearable,
withdrawing or change might be a
desirable or even mandatory de-junking
manoeuvre.

Beware of chronic junklings

There can be no valueless or
unimportant person; all human beings
have a unique make-up and deserve
respect and consideration for what they
are or have chosen to do with their lives.
But there are some people who carry so
much junk in their appearance and
lifestyle that they need only walk through
a place (or a life) to clutter it up.

We usually have a choice as to whom
we become friends and associates with. If
we link up with a person with junk
attitudes and aspirations, we'll get a junk
relationship in return.

Living to be productive and happy is a
struggle — full of tests, obstacles and
sacrifices. Those who have chosen junk
standards, who have chosen not to be
industrious, constructive or honest, have
chosen a loser's path to travel. They're not
necessarily bad people, but they're
keeping their lives like most of us keep our
belongings — with a lot of junk mixed in.
This makes interaction with them
uninspiring, if not unbearable.

The biggest problem with junk
relationships is that they occupy the time
when other, more meaningful
relationships could be enriching our lives.
A person who takes our time and emotion
in return for nothing is worse than an item
taking up physical space on our premises.
Junk people become psychological
leeches — they suck the life and energy
and enthusiasm out of us, often just by
their presence.

Like many of you, I've been a
champion of the underdog as long as I can
remember. In coaching, no matter how
inept some of those who tried to get into
the team, I had great difficulty cutting
them out of the squad. As an employer of
thousands of people, I've never found it
easy to choose the productive person and
send the one with junk ability packing.
I've financed and taken into my home
(and still do) people who have severe

problems and setbacks. If they tap hidden reserves in you, help you forge new strengths and skills neither of you realized were there — it may well be a worthwhile sacrifice on your part. But too often this is not the case; the 'problem' goes on forever till it strips and exhausts you — both your physical and financial resources and your good nature. When you can't help, if they are unwilling at this point to put effort into their own recovery — as un-brotherly or un-sisterly as this may sound, you need to rid yourself of chronic junklings. It is probably the kindest, most constructive thing you can do for them. Being thrown out of your life for a while might give them the hint to reshape a few things in theirs — and they're the only ones who can do it.

Don't let yourself be dragged down by constant association with junk people. I'm not recommending a guillotine party for all those hangers-on who've been plaguing you — only that you refuse to let them clutter your life until they show some interest (and action) in contributing to instead of confusing it. It's better to be alone than in bad company.

Crowd junkers out of your life

This is one of the positive ways to avoid junk relationships; you can enrol in a night class or fill your timetable so tight that wasteful relationships will have to fall by the wayside. Most junk relationships breed in non-constructive situations — so jog, take a second job, start your own business, or a new hobby — use the time productively somehow. When you're hanging around, you're an open invitation for others to hang on you.

Try to put them to use

Have a few unpleasant projects you need help with waiting in the wings and

launch into them when a junkee arrives. You'll get help or get rid of the unwanted guest — either way it's a plus for you. Hard work has a way of turning off junkees.

When junk friends turn up, it's simple to say, 'Hey, I'm right in the middle of this —. Would you mind sorting, shovelling, carrying, etc.?' By this means I've converted not a few misdirected visitors into productive guests.

Avoid the places junk people hang out

Trouble and time-wasting and problems take root in certain environments — like the group roaming the corridors at school or the children smoking behind the fence.

My interest in many sports and social activities was short-lived because they were infested with too many people with nothing to do and nowhere to go. So many 'haunts' suffer from the same time, same place, same old people, same old conversations syndrome; coffee breaks and other breaks are always times when tongues and brains are engaged but not to good effect. Cocktail parties are another place where people spend hours giggling, nibbling, crunching, gulping, slurping, blowing smoke and hot air in each other's faces. Country clubs, too, are clutter to a lot of people who belong.

Too much swimming pool time, pub time, party time, driving around time, theatre time leaves us without any of our own time. When we spend all our time letting people and places shape us, we don't shape ourselves or make our own mark — we miss out on some of the greatest thrills of living.

Don't join junk organisations

We owe our very history and heritage to the dedication and accomplishments of groups and organizations. But just as a single small souvenir grows into a collection, or watching a single TV game show can blossom into a something-for-nothing attitude, many organizations, groups, clubs and movements have grown into a large junk experience. There are numerous clubs and organizations that build, educate and improve life and society. But there are others that have junk meetings and conferences, play junk games, do junk projects, tell junk jokes, go to junk places, promote junk causes and help produce junk people.

I had an active college life — was in the debating society, played football, was in the Education Association; I benefited and the groups benefited. I wasn't interested in social clubs because I got all the fellowship I needed from my home and business. When I finished college we moved into a nice community, and a delegation from a well-known national organization was soon knocking on my door. I went at their invitation to an introductory social dinner, taking my wife and six children — we were the only family there amid the drift of cigarette smoke and fog of formal ceremony. I was politely informed later that this wasn't a family organization, and that was all I needed to know. It was a fine organization but my time was limited and being with my family in the evening was important. I couldn't afford nights frolicking alone when the children and I could participate together in youth club, Scouts, swimming club, PTA and other activities we enjoyed and that I felt changed lives to the good.

Because an organization exists, or even because it benefits someone else, is no indication that it is good for *you*. You know what you'd really benefit from joining, and what you wouldn't; you know the limits of your own timetable and resources.

I bet every one of you belongs to one or two (or three or four) things that are a pain to sustain and are benefiting you and the cause for which they exist very little. They must go if you intend to free your life. It takes time, energy and money to belong to the 'Thrasharound Association'. Gracefully surrender your membership. If you can't see the benefit, don't join in the first place. As is the case with most of your junk, only *you* know what must go.

Beware of the 'bored' room

Junk meetings are one of the most efficient collecting places of junk associates. When worthless meetings are cast off, so is much two-legged junk. Meetings — business, church, group, club, school, etc. — can be the biggest junk pastime in the world. People have meetings to work out when to have the next meeting.

About fifty per cent of all meetings can be de-junked; they're only held because they've been scheduled and because 'meeting' is a bona fide buzz word of the business world — no one dares question it. A business executive confided in me once that his (major) corporation had made a miraculous recovery from near-bankruptcy; they did it by firing half their managers. Oddly, they didn't miss them; business picked up! The matter was researched to see what all those hardworking managers had been doing. Guess what was found? Sixty-five per cent of their managers' time had been spent going to meetings, another 25 per cent *preparing* to go to the meetings, and the remaining 10 per cent making notes/reports on the meetings (which no one ever read).

Many meetings are just an exercise in calling to order and dismissing. Doers spend their time doing, result-getters use time to get results.

Philosophizers, consensus-seekers, and the unconfident have to hold multiple meetings to give some appearance of activity. Meetings create the unfortunate illusion that because you've *talked* about it, you've done something about it. Then everyone goes, satisfied, back to their desks — until the next meeting to *talk* about the problem. At many a meeting people simply hum and haw, show off and stall, trying to come up with something worthy to be noted, when a good leader could have made a decision and everybody could have stayed at home. We're too often afraid to stand up and say, 'This meeting is unnecessary every week,' because the word 'meeting' is hallowed. *Don't you believe it!* I run five different businesses and have served on numerous boards; I've discovered that my happiness, energy, creative ability and net worth all grew as my attendance at meetings decreased. I have about three meetings a week now instead of over twenty-five as I once had. (We do need a few meetings to communicate important information.) Too many people think 'committee' means 'meeting.' If everyone fulfils his or her assignment, a couple of meetings a year to report and evaluate is plenty.

Unclutter your life of junk meetings (you've known all along what they are), and use the time to get the work done instead of 'aying' and 'naying' over it. Democracy should be a meeting of the *minds,* not the bodies.

If all else fails, move

It has been given to us to love all man- and womankind, but sometimes we need to love at a distance for a while.

There is a difference to learn here between helping and doing. If you are always around and easily accessible, people (even your close family) will grow to depend on your strength (help, loans, transport, etc.). This can be bad in the sense that they may never develop their own strengths. In your deliberate absence, they often find out they can make things happen on their own and finally begin to build lives of accomplishment.

One last thought: maybe someone is trying to de-junk you

Is it always the other person? Could *you* be a junker? It *is* possible, you know, that you've cluttered your habits and yourself with so much junk that nobody wants you. Have you had some difficulty being wanted or needed, have you had to fight to maintain a relationship, job, assignment or position? Maybe someone is trying to de-junk you (a much scarier thought than how you're going to de-junk someone else).

Did it ever occur to you the reason people avoid you, don't employ you, don't choose you for the team, leave you behind, forget to pick you up, never ask you out or over is that maybe — just maybe — *you* are a junk friend or relative or teammate?

Junk kills the appeal of the finest things, even a human being. Maybe the TV that says gargling gives you lustier breath and skin tight jeans make you irresistible is wrong, and your junk habits of constant undependability, bad debts, foul language, criticism, crudeness, rudeness or sloppiness of appearance have turned you into a personal piece of junk. It takes more than one person to create a junk relationship.

Could man's best friend be clutter?

Sometimes clutter does creep in *literally* on the hoof, or, more frequently on paws.

Don't get me wrong — I love animals. I grew up around corrals with snorting horses, rooting pigs, pecking chickens, lovable lambs and others. I cried for weeks when my old dog Lucky was knocked down by a car. Even cats, who do little but crawl on the back of snagged chairs and look surly, I can respect. I saw to it that my kids had chicks, pups, goldfish, hamsters, gerbils, turtles, and lizards. I've even read the statistics that not one of the ten most wanted criminals ever owned a dog — but with pets, as with anything, when you overdo it, the benefits are reversed. The junk of pets can destroy the value of their ownership — or, in a pet phrase, 'the tail wags the dog.'

Have you ever put your 'pet junk' to the test?

Pet cages
Pet snacks
Pet slimming diets
Pet exercisers
Pet doors
Pet dinnerware
Pet piddle grit
Pet perfumes
Pet collar tags
Pet pills and powders
Pet toys
Pet ponchos
Pet footwear
Pet whiteners
Pet restraining devices
Pet training devices
Pet portraits
Pet family planning
Pet pedigrees (genealogy)
Pet patios
Pet swimming pools
Pet pets

What happened to the old pets that just curled up at the foot of the master's bed? Now we have to order a hand-crafted bed on wheels for them!

There are even junk breeds of animals — carefully bred to be so decorative that they're useless for anything, even pets. Nature produces excellent animals if we leave her alone — the Heinz 57 mongrel and the striped moggy are first-class mousers or all-round pets. But that isn't good enough for some junk breeders. They have to do their genetic meddling and come up with a hybrid hound that looks good with the mistress posed in a sleek slit dress — but the poor dog has no strength, no stamina, no nerve, and can't even reproduce without human help. It's too delicate to take on a hike or even to play with the children, but that pedigree makes us keep it — for what?

The funny part about pets is that the person who buys them is often not the person who really has to put up with them (change that litter, trot out in the rain for those walks, clean the tack and muck out the stall).

Remember, when you consider the value of a pet, that you want to be sure who has the leash on whom. Plain old flea collars kill fleas; diamond-studded collars draw thieves. Somewhere in between you can have a pet lead you to a better life.

Geranium junk

There is no doubt that plants give a dwelling warmth, beauty, style and the message that nature still is the greatest designer and decorator of all. Anyone

who doesn't harbour a plant or two might well be suspected of a cold streak — but it *is* possible to own so many that you can't see life through the leaves.

It was a cruelly chilly winter day when a pickup, apparently moving a family, pulled into the petrol station for fuel. The driver was barely able to see through the clump of foliage in the seat next to him. Suddenly the foliage moved — and a woman crawled out from under the plants. Some chattering from the back told us that under a mound of old blankets and quilts there were three children riding in the cold air in the open back of the truck. The service-station attendant, a father of nine, suggested to the woman that perhaps it would be more humane to put the plants in the back of the truck and let the children sit in the cab. In total sincerity she said, 'Oh, my plants would freeze, if I put them back there.'

The insidious thing about greenery junk is that you start out innocently with a small pot of forget-me-nots and they sprout into so many growths that indeed you *can't* forget them. (The general principle of plant propagation is: if you don't really care for it, it'll survive — and thrive — and multiply.) I've been in homes where the host did nothing for the three days of my visit but water and mist and clip vegetation; she couldn't go anywhere or do anything because her plants took so much care. Plants were made to enjoy, not necessarily to employ us full-time.

Most houses don't really have the right conditions for the plants we fancy — they never look anywhere near as good as they did when we brought them home crisp and fresh from the greenhouse. Soon all those brown tips and shedding leaves more depress than uplift us. And then, of course, we have to amass a plethora of preparations to treat their ailments and help them survive our basically inhospitable home environment.

Clip back some of that growth and watch the growth of human communication around you. You don't need a rain forest in your living room to get atmosphere, a plantation of pygmy palms to convince people you're a sensitive bloke — a few nice plants can do it.

Throw out all those spindly, sickly-looking specimens that make you feel guilty, or give them to a green-fingered friend who thinks there's hope. Sure, they're alive — but barely — and you can bet that whatever they feel, it's not good.

Yes, plant lovers, your darkest suspicions are correct — I'm low enough to sneak in a silk or plastic plant or two, if it might save time and trouble.

Nothing on this earth influences the quality of our life, positively or negatively, as do our relationships. Surround yourself with de-junked or sincerely de-junking people; get the junk cleaned out and your life will glow with health and love. Maintaining constructive, inspiring relationships will keep a sparkle in your eye and goose bumps on your neck.

Chapter 16

How to leave it and love it (clutter)

You wake up one morning and suddenly realise you're buried in problems. The more you think about them the more they seem to multiply. You drag yourself out into the day, through your home full of things you're struggling to pay for, things you seldom use. You get to work and see the IN tray triumphing over the OUT tray. You light a cigarette or go for a cup of coffee and a Danish pastry to help you face the work and you *still* can't face it. When you at last unearth your desk top you find the final demand for the telephone bill.

At these discouraging times, before you reach for more aspirin, a one way ticket to outer Mongolia or a shoulder to cry on, reverse it all. Decide to finally get rid of the clutter that's causing your bad day, plaguing your life and mind, clogging up your efficiency and bruising your shins. Throw out the clutter first before you swing into that miracle plan to rearrange your life for maximum efficiency, or set in motion that complicated strategy of self-improvement. It's as simple and logical as throwing away the shoes that are blistering and cramping your feet, or.

throwing out the rotten apples at the bottom of the bowl before you try to wash it out. The time you invest in de-junking will pay you back many times more — you'll save all those hours you lost making detours around, moving about, cleaning up and agonizing over junk.

It's amazing how many problems go away when junk does. Once something is eliminated, its capacity to clutter and mess up your life is gone. Your life is simplified — and you're free to concentrate on the important things instead of thrashing around in the piles of rubbish. You'll wonder why you didn't do it sooner when you realize how little effort will be needed to reorganize, restore and regain control of things. I guarantee that getting rid of your clutter is the best antidepressant there is.

You'll have a wonderful feeling of completion and accomplishment and self-mastery when you stick to an anti-clutter campaign in your life. Enjoy the most refreshing experience in the world — that great sigh of relief when you're totally (well, 95 per cent) free of all those unused possessions.

Besides, while you're de-junking you'll probably find some things you've been looking for for years — such as the flash unit for the camera, your lower dentures or the spare keys for the car.

When is the best time to throw away your clobber?

The best time to start throwing out is after you've decided that the clobber is clobber. If you wait for further confirmation, you'll fall back in love with the clutter in your life and keep it. To be more specific, here are some guidelines reported by successful de-junkers.

Morning
Light beats darkness for evaluating things. You're more objective in the morning, have more energy to go through the clutter and to throw out what you don't need. The earlier the better — a 5.00 a.m. session is exhilarating. Choose the morning the refuse collectors call so

that afterwards, when you start wishing you hadn't got rid of it all, it'll be too late.

Sundays, holidays and long weekends
These are probably the best times to reflect, analyse and file, to review your values and strip yourself of burdens (90 per cent of your burdens are rubbish-related).

Autumn
As the trees shed their leaves at the end of the season, so should you shed some of your worn and tired treasures. It's time to store some, sell some and get rid of the rest so they won't weigh on your mind and depress you all winter. Besides, you're going to collect more over Christmas and you'll need some room for them.

On a few of those brisk autumn days or evenings, instead of going out stay at home and get rid of some of the things you no longer need. You'll find it entertaining and exhilarating, and it won't give you a hangover.

Mood
It's quite effective to go through your clutter when you're angry — we need to take aggression out on something. We get through the housework quickly and effectively when we're hopping mad about something and it's when we're angry that we're the least sentimental. However, if you're so cross that you're full of disdain for someone (or something) you'll often not make good decisions and will be sorry later (and maybe have to charge off to the dump to try to get something back). If you're experiencing a peak of energy and motivation, make the most of it. Roll up your sleeves and start on the piles of useless possesion.

Age
Eight years old is probably the time to start individual accountability for your

belongings and the older you are the more time you will have had to amass unwanted possessions.

Today

Now is probably the best time to start. Don't wait until all your storage space is taken up or until someone is threatening to leave you before you start de-junking. Don't get pushed into doing it when you haven't time to do it properly.

What to wear

When de-junking, never wear clothes with big pockets which may tempt you to pop things into them. And if you're going through the stuff for the second time, wear dark glasses! Sturdy, low-heeled shoes are a good idea, and make sure you wear something you won't be afraid of getting messy.

Should you go it alone?

Most of us don't like friends or companions to meddle in our beloved clutter, but when we're overcome by the amount of clutter we have and reach the depths of depression, we will perhaps find it advantageous to have someone standing by when we seize something and hold it up to weigh its worth. They'll probably say one of two things:

'Good grief! Whatever do you keep that old thing for?' And it's final — out it goes! Or, as their greedy eyes light up:

'Ooohhh! *I'll* have that!' And again, it's gone for good.

If de-junking gets to be too emotional an undertaking, reformed junkees say that it's helpful to find another struggling junkee and do a swap. Let them have a go at your cupboards and you have a go at theirs. It's easy to de-clutter someone else's house: you can be as objective as a forester roaming a forest marking trees to be felled. You are only using your expertise to identify; you

don't have to actually throw anyone else's clutter out. Just label or mark it and the decisions are made. But you'll probably have to accept some of the labels on *your* treasures.

One of the biggest disadvantages of being a junkee is that your reputation as a hoarder will inspire friends to bring anything they don't want to you, thinking they're doing you a favour.

Discount what you can't count

One division of my contract cleaning business handles cleaning up after fire and flood damage. In each case the victim of the fire or other disaster is asked to make a list of the items in the attic, basement or other room that was destroyed. To most people that's like asking them to memorize the Bible. They know the cupboards, trunks and drawers were full, but of what? There follows a week of feverish mental activity, trying to list everything for the proof of loss. It proves that a lot of it must have been junk if they can't remember it.

Making a list of all you own and where it is is a sensible thing to do — start in one room and go through everything. Soon you'll find things not worth the ink or effort to write down and you'll throw them away.

Pace yourself

Rome wasn't de-junked in a day. Two drawers a day is an honourable accomplishment; two drawers and a cupboard is pushing the limit; six drawers and a workshop/attic/garage could be suicidal. If you try to do too much at once you'll lose your edge and not be nearly fierce enough to get the job done properly.

Pace yourself; don't get side tracked. When you start to clear out an area get the job *done*. Otherwise when you go to throw out that old baking tray you'll notice on the way to the dust-bin that the back garden needs de-junking. So you stop to do the garden but notice the toolshed is in a mess. You stop to tidy the toolshed and find that the plants on the patio need repotting and it suddenly occurs to you that the baking tray you were taking to the dust-bin is just the thing to put under the plant pots. So nothing gets thrown out.

How to get rid of it

Simply throwing out your unwanted possessions is harsh and not always the best or the wisest way to dispose of them. You really should sort them out and here is a good method to follow:

Start with three large heavy-duty refuse bags and one box. Label them.

Dragging your bags and box behind you, systematically attack every room in the house. Assign every piece of loose clutter, clothing, magazines, toys, shoes, etc. to one of the bags or the box.

Everything in the Junk bag must be thrown away.

CHARITY
If it's still repairable or useful (to someone else), or it's the wrong colour, style or size, pop it into the charity bag. Let someone else worry about it for a change.

Everything in the Charity bag should be good, i.e. it can be used by someone; it could raise money for some cause; (but it won't be used by you!)

Take it to an Oxfam shop or a similar charity shop, so that it can be sold to someone who will use it and will raise much needed money to help the world's poor.

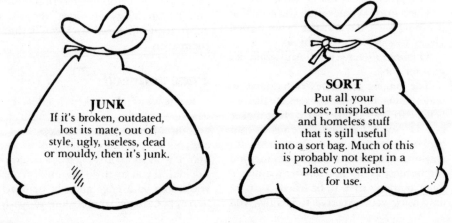

JUNK
If it's broken, outdated, lost its mate, out of style, ugly, useless, dead or mouldy, then it's junk.

SORT
Put all your loose, misplaced and homeless stuff that is still useful into a sort bag. Much of this is probably not kept in a place convenient for use.

In the Sort bag you should put things you want but have nowhere to keep. Leave the bag for a while. The longer you leave it, the less you miss whatever is in it. Finally, the dread of sorting it outweighs the dread of throwing it away and, after taking out the things you really do need, it's three bags down and one to go!

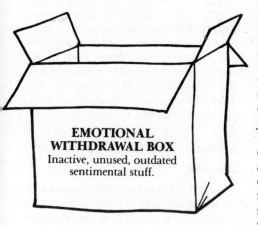

EMOTIONAL WITHDRAWAL BOX
Inactive, unused, outdated sentimental stuff.

Into the Emotional Withdrawal box go all those items which you honestly can't bring yourself to throw away. That shortie nightie you wore on your honeymoon, that little memento from your child's first school trip... Don't upset yourself and lose momentum by trying to argue with your emotions. Just pat the article affectionately and lay it gently in your Emotional Withdrawal box. Write the date in huge letters on the box and store it somewhere safe. Then, six months from the date on the box (or a year if you're really sentimental), retrieve the box. Do not open it or peek into it. By now you've forgotten what it was you put in there. Or you *do* remember but that gripping moment of emotional attachment has passed and you can dispassionately deliver the box to the nearest charity shop or drag it out to the pavement on dustbin day. You won't feel a thing except victory — and pleasure — over your tidy cupboards and spacious storage areas.

Throw it right out

When you throw out things make sure you do it thoroughly. As with weeding a garden there can be no half measures. Throw it away, give it away or sell it, but get *rid* of it! As with pulling off sticking plaster it hurts less if you do it quickly and decisively. Failure to do so may result in a severe case of junkitis. The fatal day comes when you take your stuff to a jumble sale and just stay for a quick look. You'll see something there you really could use — an old sweatshirt just right for a car rag, for example — so in goes one bit of rubbish and out comes another. How much credit will you get for that? Not much! And next time you'll be *looking* and you'll drag home more than you took. That's how junkitis progresses.

The only way to stop this affliction getting a hold on you is to keep telling yourself all the way to the dustbin or charity shop how loathsome the things you are doing away with are. If you know you'll weaken or come home with something someone else was throwing away, ask someone strong-minded to go with you. Or pay a neighbour's child to do it for you. Be ruthless! Better still, stop the accumulation of clutter by employing the 'one in, one out' rule, meaning if you bring anything new into your home, something old has to be removed.

Beware the senseless spree

It's possible to be a de-junking fanatic. Remember, the adage 'One man's junk is

131

another man's treasure' does have some truth to it. As our lives and environments change they affect what and how much we need. You should find a happy medium for giving, swapping, throwing away or keeping.

One repentant fanatic I know got a six-slice toaster for a wedding present; she threw it in the bin, still in the unopened box. In a few years toasters were twice the price and there were five in her family instead of two. Think ahead; your circumstances may change. There's always room to store genuinely useful things.

Going on a complete binge and throwing out tons of stuff is thoughtless and wasteful.

Recycling – the great equalizer

Much of our clutter can be recycled, and even if we get little or no cash for it we can help clean up the environment,

contribute to the economy and make ourselves feel good into the bargain. Just think, those old clothes, newspapers, tins and tyres we've been stumbling over for years can be reincarnated into a warm quilt, an elegant greetings card, shiny sheet metal or a football. Glass, paper, cardboard, tin foil, iron, aluminium, old cars, dirty motor oil, car batteries and numerous other materials can be pulped, stripped down, melted and turned into re-usable commodites. Check with your local council refuse department to see exactly what they handle; it is different in different parts of the country. If they haven't placed bottle banks in your area, urge them to do so.

A positive future for your clutter

Even if *you* don't want and never will want a particular article, it is always possible, if it is still in good useful condition, that someone will pay a reasonable sum for it. So often tools, equipment, clothes, work or play things are still good when we no longer need them. But then, forgetting that their only value was in actual use, we feel an obligation to preserve them, as if we were trying to preserve the part of our lives they touched. Don't turn them from a positive into a negative. They weren't rubbish, but we can turn them into rubbish by keeping them hanging around. Use those classified ads and let someone else enjoy the things which once gave you pleasure. But, better still, if you aren't desperate for the money, collect all the things that are of dubious value to you and donate them to a worthy cause. Oxfam shops are an excellent outlet. It is a sad fact that while most of us in the affluent West are drowning in our own possessions, bogged down and even depressed by the ownership of so many objects, the majority of the earth's population not only have no possessions at all, but do not even have adequate housing or clothing. Some of these people, to the lasting shame of the human race, do not have enough food. Oxfam exists to do whatever its supporters make possible to remedy this unjust imbalance. There are now 660 Oxfam shops in the UK, run by volunteers, and more will be opening over the next three years. They are pleased to receive bric à brac, jewellery, good, wearable clothing, household equipment (in working order and not too large); in fact anything that will sell. In 1983 Oxfam shops alone raised over £8,000,000. There is probably one near you so take your goods along and they can be turned into money — money which could be vital to the survival of a child somewhere in the Third World.

De-junking is not forever

De-junking is a journey, not a destination; a process, not an end product. You don't get rid of your clutter and stay tidy forever, because new junk will keep filtering in to fill the vacancies. It's like fitness or cleanliness — it doesn't last; de-junking from time to time must become a reflex action. Be on the look out for junk danger zones. If you're a one time junkee remember that your very worst enemies are: moving into a bigger house; reading junk 'pornography' ('things and possessions' catalogues — see chapter 8); reading a '101-things-to-make-out-of-junk' book. Be ever watchful — be strict with yourself.

Chapter 17

Let's get started on your clutter

There are many possible solutions to clutter.

1. You could *have your clutter cremated* and have a daily or weekly viewing of the vase containing the remains, if deep feelings are still there for your junk. It can remain with you, in spirit and condensed form.

2. You could *microfilm it* and carry every bit of your junk everywhere you go.

3. You can *seal it up in the cornerstone* of your new house, and it will finally have value when it's dug out centuries later — as an archaeological find.

4. Our modern computers might be the ultimate solution to the modern-day problem of junk. With a computer you have two choices for keeping track of your junk.

   a You can simply *program all your junk onto a disc* — what, where, when you last saw it, etc. — and when you get a longing for it you can call up that file so you'll know exactly where it is.

   b Or even more useful (because we seldom actually use junk), you can *program all your junk into a visual format* and then get rid of it. Then when you feel the need to have a look at it you can press computer recall — and there it is to radiate security and be enjoyed, while taking up no appreciable room.

5. *You can do nothing*. Actually, doing absolutely nothing about the junk that has overcome you is the most common aproach. This is also called retreat. It is totally chicken-hearted; you will retreat again and again, and junk will multiply.

6. *Retrench*. When any of your junk — things or personal habits — threatens you and your comfort zone, you hide it in a better place, pack it in tighter, contain it like nuclear waste so it won't contaminate its surroundings — thus we become slaves, servants, flunkies to junk.

7. *Planned clearance*. Might facing up to junk be the best solution?

Well then — let's get started!

Judging junk

Anything that crowds the life out of you is junk. Anything that enriches your spirit — that makes you truly happy, regardless of how worthless it may be in cash terms — isn't junk. Something worth £100,000 can be pure clutter to you if it causes discomfort and anxiety or insulates you from love or a relationship.

Most active things are not junk, most inactive things are. But you have to determine the degree of activity that makes something meaningful to you. Whatever contributes to a happy, free, resourceful, sharing life isn't junk to you — but it might be one day. Our needs and values change — with our age, location, mates and degree of self-development. We should keep our eyes on the new horizon of life coming and that means that some of the tools, places and things we used in the old life, although once good and valuable, might now be junk. As we reach out and grow up, we have to learn to throw out.

The American pioneers provide us with an excellent example of this. Heading west, they loaded up all their possessions and precious treasures — including heavy hand-carved furniture, elaborate table settings, trunks of clothes, decorative gates and headboards and oversized clocks.

When they reached the rough-hewn trails and steep terrain of the hills they were forced, if they were to survive, to lighten their loads, to discard some of their good stuff; it was, although costly, clutter to them at that moment. Others coming along the trail found the valuables free for the taking, but they too had to judge it as junk (and leave it behind) because it stood in the way of their greatest goal — their destiny. So it is with junk: that which restricts our living, loving, thinking and feeling is junk, be it a thing, habit, person, place or position. You alone have to make this judgment, because only you fully understand your position in life, your goals, your emotional ties, the time you have available and the limitations of your physical self and space.

Consider the story of a family travelling by car on a long holiday to the south of France. At one of the first gift shops the father shook a wise bony finger at his three travel-weary children and said, 'Now don't you kids buy any junk with your hard-earned money, do you hear?' The

children bought some chocolate, a 95p book of word games, a cheap metal ring and one of those paper birds that fly.

While the parents lingered in the gift shop, the children went out on the freshly mown lawn, wound the bird up, and threw it back and forth, screaming with delight, running, jumping, laughing and breathing the fresh country air. At every stop they did it. The paper bird was the finest thing going. As they drove along they did the word searches — and everyone felt and examined the 'real' turquoise ring. In four days that bird provided those children with more exposure to nature and good feelings than they'd had for a long time. On the fifth day, the bird, tattered and torn, gave up the ghost.

When the children got back into the car, the parents turned on them and said, 'You stupid kids, that's what you get for buying junk, what do you have now for your money, the word game book is all done, the bird is broken, and that ring, if you keep passing it around, will soon be lost. Spend your money on something nice like we did. You'll have something to show for your holdiay.' (The parents at the same stop had bought four cups of coffee, a varnished wall plaque that contained the words 'ass', 'hell' and 'damn', a £2.50 women's glamour magazine and an ugly carved ivory figurine.) The children, with downcast eyes, felt guilty and learned there and then that one of the main purposes of a holiday is to bring back stuff (junk). The children's stuff wasn't junk — it enhanced, stimulated and accelerated their feelings for each other and the beautiful country they were travelling through. The parents' figurine was packed away and hidden — it had no value; the paper bird beat it a hundred times over. *Junk depends on your use of something, and what it does to your life.*

Don't let hard-earned cash buy you a hard head!

I wanted a top quality slide projector. My expert camera man sold me a handsome model and twenty trays to go with it. The unit, impressive as the name engraved on it might be in other circumstances, was a flop — a failure of design. I got annoyed and then angry with it and badgered the company to make it work. *They* were so fed-up with that model, they'd stopped making it — or parts for it. But do you think I could get them to take back that bright mechanical dinosaur and all its accessories? No, and twelve years later I gave it to my son-in-law, who is now beating and kicking and cursing it and trying to decide what to do with twenty expensive-looking slide trays.

One of the biggest reasons we keep junk is that we hate to admit mistakes. Often we acquire a thing, a job, a habit that we absolutely hate the minute after we get it. But we don't get round to taking it back (or leaving, or stopping), though it's a constant pain to maintain, to own, to be around. In general it makes life miserable but we keep it — why? Because we don't want to admit we were wrong or greedy for a moment or made a bad judgment.

There's nothing wrong with making mistakes — cautious living and five accomplishments only get five things experienced a week. Only those who wade in and do fifty things a week and make twenty mistakes get thirty experiences to the good and gain confidence; they generally end up years ahead in living and enjoying life. Mistakes can be tolerated as experiences which contribute to your personal growth, but don't hold on to your mistakes — throw out the evidence!

Don't be prejudiced by pride

It was a cool morning and I was dressed for a hike in the hills, when a wiser and older man I barely knew came up to me and said, 'You ought to take that last heavy coat off, you aren't going to need it, and you'll get hot later.' Like any other twenty-five-year-old I knew how to dress, and what business was it of his? I resented him questioning my decision — so I wore it. Half a mile up the hill, I knew I'd made a mistake, but decided to pretend I was enjoying being overwarm. One hour later the sun was beating down and I was heating up like a pressure cooker. I still hated to admit that his suggestion to take off the coat back at the car was right, so I suffered for another hour. I was so dehydrated I felt like a shrivelled hide when, about three that afternoon, some people passed heading back to the camp and asked if they could take the coat back to lighten my load. Humbler than I was in the morning, I gave them the coat and immediately began to enjoy a bright, beautiful, carefree afternoon in the mountains.

When you find yourself resenting having to, or being told to throw something away or give something up, consider first and foremost the reward, the end result — how you and your life will be without it. Nothing is more stimulating than being rid of something or habit that has held you down. When you pause with the decision in mind or hand — shall it go or shall it stay with you — when logic and even emotion can't manage to help you reach a decision; ask

yourself, 'What will my life be like without this?' Don't think about *it* (the thing) — think about *you*, your life, your freedom.

Some junk-sorting guidelines

Is it clutter or is it not? Is your de-junking fever being cooled down by cold feet? Are emotional ties and guilt diluting your ability to be ruthless and strong? If indecisiveness sets in, here are some guidelines that may help.

It is junk if:
- it's broken or obsolete (and mending it is unrealistic)
- you've outgrown it, physically or emotionally
- you've always hated it
- it's the wrong size, wrong colour or wrong style
- using it is more bother than it's worth
- it wouldn't really matter if you never saw it again
- it generates bad feelings
- you have to clean it, store it and insure it (but you don't get much use or enjoyment out of it)
- it will shock, bore or burden the next generation.

If you can tick one or more of the above truthfully, then it's probably junk. Do yourself, your house and posterity a favour — throw it out! It's robbing you of peace of mind and space.

It's not junk if it:
- generates love and good feelings
- helps you make a living
- will do something you need done
- has significant cash value
- gives you more than it takes

- will enrich or delight the coming generation

If you can tick a few of the above comfortably, then it's probably *not* junk — enjoy it and feel good about its place in your life.

Clutter's last stand

The *real* fate worse than death is the probability that what we are now, we'll remain for the rest of our lives.

We can change our looks, the place we live in, job and economic position, but what we are as people, we'll remain if the things, places, people that made us that way stay with us. The anxieties, unhappiness, discomfort and disgust we're struggling with now might shift position but will remain with us, keeping us the same.

It's discouraging to think that a load of clutter could cheat us out of our future — a vibrant, zestful, rapture-filled life. It can! It *is*!

But we can have it all back, revive, restore, re-experience those fine fun feelings and love if we allow some room for them. Right now that room in our homes and hearts is piled with clutter — some we loaded in, some we absorbed, some that was dumped on or given to us. But how it got there doesn't matter nearly as much as how we're going to get rid of it.

Life doesn't begin at forty, sixty-five, twenty, thirty, when we get married, when we get promoted, or when we have grandchildren — life really begins when we discover how flexible and free we are without clutter.

Remember, any junk or clutter (house clutter, car clutter, mind clutter) can and will sprout into more of the same. We humans wrinkle and wither fast, mentally and physically, from the burden of

worthless cargo.

Deciding what is clutter may be our own opinion, but whether or not we keep it in our lives may not be strictly our own business. Because we can be sure that some way, someday, somehow, even right now, our clutter will not only hurt us, but drastically affect the lives of others.

Clutter is simply undealt-with junk. Usable things are used, valuable things contribute value, you'll seldom find good things cluttering life — it's the non- or little-needed things that are hung onto for the sheer sake of owning and having. How long it stands and mows you down is up to you alone. *Freedom from clutter* will free the years, the months, the weeks, the days and the hours you've spent hauling, digging, wallowing, sorting, hunting, protecting in the past. With the clutter will go the mess you've battled with all your life — and defeating clutter will cost you nothing but a decision.

Remember, everything costs something to acquire and to maintain. The majority of this cost you pay with your time and energy. To lead the life you really want to lead, you must eliminate the clutter and excess from your mind, home, and habits. It's simple, and one of the easiest ways to be 'born again'.

Clearing out the excess in your life is the cheapest, fastest, and most effective way of becoming physically and financially sound, emotionally and intellectually happy.

Clearing out the excess in your life will really raise your standard of living, give you back the life that clutter stole from you.

I've tried to give you physical, financial, emotional and aesthetic reasons to de-junk your life.

I'm hoping I've managed to give you a few strong hints on how, where and when to begin de-junking. There is a time to stop war-dancing and circling around our junk and to attack it! A time to make our junk tremble in the trenches instead of us cowering from its clutter. Losing a few old habits and heirlooms might leave a tiny wound or two, but *you'll win! You'll conquer! You'll be free!* No blood will spill from your defeated junk — but blood will again begin to flow for life instead of for objects.

Attack with the strength of a lion: start grabbing those junk items that have been smothering you, competing for your time and affection, costing you money and concern, and throw them out, give them away, donate them, sell them, burn them — anything — but get them out of your sight and mind. Ignore the outcries of onlookers who have to crawl out from under their junk to give you reasons to cling on forever.

As the clutter goes, light will penetrate to you and then you can de-junk in a big way — ten times faster than you accumulated it. The fresh air of relief, of living will begin to envelop you, the exhilaration of true power and control will permeate your being.

Once you've de-junked you won't accumulate again as fast; you'll automatically have a built-in new sense of value that will inspire you to spot clutter and avoid it. The junk will seem to disintegrate by itself — people will give

you less (if any), you won't buy any. You won't believe how naturally it works!

Start now — The older you are, the more you have to de-junk. And the longer you've been suffering from junk, the happier you'll be when you've de-junked!

Thanks for buying and reading this book — I appreciate it. And thanks to all the people who contributed 'junk wisdom' to these pages.

The final judgment

Let me repeat: I'm not claiming the position of the Lord Chief Justice of Junk-Judging. I'm presenting some views (perhaps tinged with a little personal opinion) to help stimulate new thoughts in your hoarding soul — but the decision of what to keep and what to get rid of is all yours. Age, sentiment, and 'I may need it one day' all have their legitimacy. Think about a fire extinguisher — it fits many of the criteria of clutter as it hangs there for twenty years. It's not the latest style, it's ugly, it never moves, it's never used, it costs money to have checked and re-checked — but it's certainly worth having when it's needed *once* in that twenty years!

The ultimate evaluation is up to you. I've shared my observations and others' contributions in this volume, but what is and is not clutter is for you to determine — by the use and benefit an item is to you, the actions it encourages you to take, and the effect it has through you on others. A piece of refuse isn't junk if it enriches the quality of life. And a beautiful, valuable and expensive thing can be total junk if it detracts from your joy of living and loving.

Have you read Don Aslett's other books?

Is There a Speech Inside You? *Hardback £9.99.* If anyone is qualified to write a book on making speeches, it's Don Aslett. In the last few years, he's given over 8,000 speeches in the USA, Britain and Australia. He's appeared time and again on national TV shows and radio; he's spoken to thousands of people at conventions, and at small community meetings to an audience of less than a dozen. The first time he spoke in public, he dried up completely. Yet he has learnt from those early difficulties and become a humorous and much sought-after speaker.

In this carefully structured guide, Don shows in his lively way that you *can* conquer your fears and become a successful speaker. In easy-to-follow stages, he takes you through preparing and researching your speech, timing and pacing, getting in tune with your audience, using visual aids, distractions and hostility, and much, much more. Whether you're going to have to make a speech at a wedding, give a series of business presentations, or want to become a professional speaker, this original and helpful guide is one you must read.

Is There Life After Housework? *Paperback £3.99.*
Over 75,000 sold in the United Kingdom.
This is the book that started it all. Don sets out to prove to everyone that 'long, grinding, unrewarding hours of toil are not necessary' to achieve a spotless and gleaming house. Don Aslett started cleaning to pay for university and has now spent over 35 years running a huge and successful contract cleaning business. He is an expert in cost-cutting and time-saving methods of cleaning, while still producing a superb result. He promises you can save up to 75 per cent of your cleaning time if you follow his advice.

All his ideas are tried and tested – he never recommends any product or method which has not been thoroughly tested out by his 2,000 cleaners – and the book contains a detailed list of suppliers of the equipment and products which Don recommends. If this book does not revolutionise your housework, you either like spending time cleaning or you employ someone else to do your dirty work.

How to Win at Housework. *Hardback £7.99, paperback £3.99.*
Over 25,000 sold in Great Britain
Don's first book was such a success that he kept being asked to lecture on cleaning techniques. He always has a question and answer session at the end of his talks and soon found that the same problems came up over and over again. This book contains the one hundred problems raised most often and Don's solutions to them. So if you can't decide whether to dust or vacuum first, need to get chewing gum out of your carpet, want to clean your extractor fan or find the grout on your bathroom tiles has gone grey, this book will help you with these (and ninety-six other) problems.

Who Says It's a Woman's Job to Clean? *Hardback, £7.99, paperback £3.99.* Now this book is controversial. It starts from the position that men, as a species, get away with murder when it comes to the daily chores of life. Even the most helpful only do the 'high profile' tasks like decorating, maintenance or possibly cooking. They run a mile from the unspeakable mess behind the fridge or from wiping down the toilets.

But no longer. Don lists all the male excuses – and demolishes them one by one. He runs the ultimate 'Macho Man Quiz' to show just how little they're really doing. Then he proceeds to show men how they *can* play fair with a crash course on cleaning. He also points out the areas where their superior strength and height gives them positive advantages. This book is fun, practical and essential reading for men. However the publishers accept no responsibility whatsoever for the divorce rate....

Other Interesting Books from Exley:
Play As We Go. *Hardback £7.99, paperback £3.99.* Most parents dread taking children on long journeys because of the boredom factor. However, with this book to hand, this should never be a problem again. Packed with games and small-scale activities for children ranging from three to thirteen, this book should keep them amused for hours and prevent fraying tempers all round.

Sing As We Go. *Hardback £7.99, paperback £3.99.* A collection of really popular songs for the family or school to sing on journeys, sing-songs or other times when you need to amuse yourselves. You should know the tunes for practically all these standard favourites.

Help! I've Got a Kid! *Hardback £7.99.* Even the best and most caring of parents will find there comes a point when their child becomes a problem and that they are having constant battles over bedtimes, food, fighting with other children or any number of other unpleasant behaviours. This book will help you understand why your child is behaving like this and how to respond positively so that your child is guided into learning good habits. Cleverly illustrated with cartoons to show effective and ineffective approaches to particular problems.

These books make super presents. Order them from your local bookseller or from Exley Publications Ltd, Dept BP, 16 Chalk Hill, Watford, Herts WD1 4BN. (Please send £1.00 to cover post and packing.) Exley Publications reserves the right to show new retail prices on books which may vary from those previously advertised.